REMOTE CONTROLLED
REAL ESTATE RICHES

REMOTE CONTROLLED

REAL ESTATE RICHES

THE BUSY PERSON'S GUIDE TO REAL ESTATE INVESTING

ADIEL GOREL

PROGRESS PRESS
San Rafael, California

Remote Controlled Real Estate Riches
© 2001 by Adiel Gorel

Progress Press
101 Lucas Valley Rd., Suite 130
San Rafael, CA 94903

ISBN 0-9707849-0-2

Printed in the United States of America

Cover Design by Cathleen Miller

For Ed Borgeson
and the memory of Connie Borgeson,
my first property managers
and dear friends

CONTENTS

FOREWORD

IF YOU'RE LIKE MOST AMERICANS, YOU'RE TOO BUSY EARNING a living to get rich. When you add the demands of home and family it's amazing that you've got time left over to do anything at all, much less think about your financial future.

Perhaps this scenario sounds familiar: you and your spouse are in your early forties, and have two children. You've read about escalating college expenses and you're worried. Your parents are retired and may need your financial support in the coming years. You'd like to retire yourself in 20 years or so, and it's suddenly occurred to you (in those few spare minutes between work, school plays, soccer games and taking the dog to the vet) that it's going to take a lot more than your income to meet all these demands.

For some people, panic sets in. They imagine that the only way they're going to get ahead is to make a small fortune...preferably overnight.

Real estate books and videos that promise quick riches take advantage of the alarm you may feel when you contemplate your future. In real estate particularly, you may be told that you can find a "perfect deal" that's going to make you wealthy. All you have to do is locate a bargain property that's worth twice what you offer, and sell it for a huge profit. 20 years can go by before a deal like that comes around, if it ever does. You can waste years trying to become an overnight millionaire—years you could have spent actually becoming a millionaire.

Between work, family and (hopefully) an occasional vacation, how are you going to find that bargain property and the "perfect" deal? It's not surprising that many potential real estate investors simply give up. Real estate get-rich-quick schemes may seem enticing at first, but it soon becomes clear that in order to reap the promised rewards, you have to become as expert as the experts, which means devoting your life to your investments.

But who has the time for that? More to the point, who wants to?

It is possible to build wealth through real estate, and it isn't contingent upon overnight success, finding the "perfect" deal or becoming an expert. *Remote Controlled Real Estate Riches* is a book for those who have no interest in giving up their current career, or even all their nights and weekends, to play the real estate game. For those who prefer to put their family, work and life first, while keeping their investments on track with a minimum expenditure of time. *Remote Controlled Real Estate Riches* will show you that you don't have to spend your weekends hunting down bargain properties, managing tenants, collecting rent, or repairing the proverbial leaky toilet in order to make safe, sound real estate investments that will secure your financial future.

In the past fifteen years, I've worked with hundreds of people just like you and purchased thousands of homes for investors and myself. I've learned the rules of successful, "hands-off" real estate investing, and distilled them down to a simple, streamlined method that's proven itself again and again. Anyone can benefit from my experience and the experience of other investors and use this method to build a real estate portfolio that will have a profound impact on his or her family's financial well-being.

I'll tell you what to buy, where to buy, and how to buy real estate in a fashion that's manageable within the framework of your busy lifestyle. I'll show you how to get started, how to make a plan based on your current commitments and future needs, and how to work with real estate professionals so that your most valuable resource—your time—is not wasted.

I'm not going to tell you that you can make a million dollars overnight, with your first deal, or even within the first year (although I know a number of investors who have). But with *Remote Controlled Real Estate Riches*, you'll discover that creating financial abundance while living the life you want is something that you can accomplish, regardless of your present circumstances.

1

EVERYONE NEEDS AN INVESTMENT PLAN (YES, EVEN YOU)

IN THE FILM THE GRADUATE, AN OLDER MAN TAPS THE YOUNG hero on the shoulder and offers some sage advice: "I've got one thing to say to you: plastics."

In 1968, this wasn't bad counsel. Since the film ends after Benjamin Braddock rescues Elaine Robinson from a loveless marriage, we'll never know if he secured his future with a career in plastics, or founded an ecologically friendly and extremely profitable recycling firm. But we all know that Ben wasn't thinking about the future much. In fact, he spent most of his time trying to avoid thinking about it.

Fortunately for Ben, he was a character in a movie.

You and I don't have the same good fortune. After we win the heart of the woman or man of our dreams, life goes on, and usually gets a lot more complicated. So what I'm going to do first is give you a figurative tap on the shoulder and offer some sage advice.

I've got one thing to say to you: financial planning.

Financial planning? What, you may wonder, does that have to do with real estate investing?

Everything. *Remote Controlled Real Estate Riches* isn't about a mythical pot of gold at the end of the rainbow. It's about creating the life you want while living the life you like. It's about building wealth so that your future is everything you want it to be.

The Empty Channel

Each of us lives in two channels: one where we work, live, earn and spend, and another where we build for the future with savings and investments. For many, the second channel is nearly empty. It's not surprising, because most of us weren't taught much about investing. Words like financial goals and retirement plan seem to belong to Wall Street experts, not us. In today's world, however, these are words you need to become familiar with; the sooner you begin, the better off you'll be.

In 1981, I came to the U.S. to finish my graduate studies in electrical engineering at Stanford University. I was here on a scholarship, so I was a poor student. When I finished graduate school, I got a job at Hewlett-Packard Laboratories near-by.

Two things happened when I got my first job. First, I felt rich all of sudden, because there was a big difference between my scholarship stipend and a Silicon Valley engineer's salary. Second, many of my colleagues had been there for 10 or 15 years. This was an interesting thing for me to see. Almost without exception, they didn't have much to show for those long years of work. Although they were well paid, they didn't have much in terms of their financial net worth. Typically they owned a home, two cars, and a 401(k).

I saw immediately that with their salary and their credit, they could have been financially independent after 15 or 20 years. Why hadn't they? Because no one had shown them that it was possible, if only they'd thought about the future, and created a financial plan of their own.

Especially for those of you who hate to balance your checkbook, the words "financial" and "planning" in tandem can be as welcome as a visit to the dentist. There are certain things in life that almost no one likes to do. Taxes, for instance. Of course, if you don't pay your taxes, you could wind up in prison. As things stand, no one's going to throw you in jail for lack of a little financial planning, so it's a lot easier to overlook.

But I'm here to tell you that financial planning is as important as sending in your tax return each year. Without it, you won't end up in jail, but you might end up in a place you don't want to be: 65, retired, and living on a small, fixed income.

Regardless of your specific goals, one aspect of financial planning is the same for all of us, and that's retirement planning. Even if retirement seems, at present, a long way off, there will come a time when you no longer wish to—or can't—work any more.

Retirement in the New Millennium

Do you remember when your grandfather retired? Chances are, when he turned 65, the company where he'd worked for 40 years threw him a party and gave him a gold watch. He received a pension that, along with Social Security benefits, allowed him to live comfortably in his "golden years."

I think I'm safe in assuming that this kind of retirement isn't in your future. We all know that life has changed enormously in the past 30 years. In 1970, the things we now take for granted—personal computers, VCRs, cell phones, microwave ovens—belonged in a Jetson's cartoon, not in our homes. While the technological innovations of the late 20th century are the most obvious indicators of change, our lifestyle has changed dramatically, too. And one of the most dramatic areas of change is in how—and how well—we'll retire.

If you're just beginning to realize that your retirement years might be less "golden" than you'd like, you have a lot of company. Anyone born after 1945—the Baby Boomer generation and beyond—is facing a vastly different future from that of their parents and grandparents. We can't rely on employers or the government to provide for us once we stop working. If we don't do it ourselves, it won't happen.

What Pension?

The truth is that most of us don't stick around for the gold watch. Careers are more often made by changing companies rather than climbing one corporate ladder; mergers and downsizing also add to frequent job changes.

401(k) retirement plans have taken the place of many

company pension plans. While a 401(k) has the benefit of moving with you when you change jobs, it also means that half the contributions come from your paycheck. The increasing numbers of free-lancers, entrepreneurs, and consultants don't even have the advantage of an employer's 50% contribution; they must rely solely on their own contributions to a government-sponsored retirement plan.

If you start contributing to a 401(k) or Keogh in your twenties or early thirties, you can conceivably amass enough wealth to be fairly comfortable when you retire—but no matter how much you put aside, inflation can wreak havoc with your nest egg. Unfortunately, I've found that most people don't even begin thinking about retirement until they're in their forties...and perhaps not even then.

Social Security

There's a very good chance that what worked for our parents and grandparents isn't going to work for us. Currently, Social Security provides a maximum of $14,000 per year— and that's only if you contributed the maximum amount during your lifetime.

I couldn't live on $14,000 per year, could you? And due to the changing demographics of our society, these benefits aren't likely to increase much. 10 years from now, Baby Boomers will begin retiring en masse and only 2 workers will be paying in for every retiree who's taking out. Unless there are drastic changes in the system, Social Security will not provide you with a comfortable retirement, unless you enjoy clipping coupons and buying groceries with food stamps.

Longer Life Spans

In 1970, the average life expectancy was 60 to 65. In fact, the entire Social Security system was based upon this life span. It meant that benefits would be paid out to only some individuals, and then only for a few years.

Today's average life expectancy is closer to 80. And who knows what the next 20 years will bring? Healthier lifestyles, medical advances, and biotechnology could easily push the average up to 100.

This is an enormously important thing to consider. It means that if you retire at 65, you may need enough money to live on for 20, 30 or even 40 years.

If you're thinking, "I'm going to need a lot of money," you're right. Not only will it have to be a lot, it will have to be inflation-proof.

Inflation

Currently, the government estimates that the annual rate of inflation is approximately 3%. If you remember the double-digit inflation of the early 1980s, it doesn't sound so bad, does it?

Think again. When prices rise 3% year after year, your purchasing power is cut by a third in only 10 years. That means that your $40,000 annual salary will be worth only $26,666 a decade hence. At a 4% rate of inflation, it will be cut in half in 18 years; at 6%, that $40,000 will be worth only $20,000 in 12 years.

It's startling, isn't it? But official statistics don't tell the whole story. Some things—education, housing and health-care—have risen much more than the average rate of inflation. When all goods and services are factored in, many experts estimate the true inflation rate at 5%. As an example, let's look at some consumer prices over the years:

CONSUMER PRICES 1960 - 2020			
	1960	1980	2000	2020 (estimated)
Loaf of Bread	0.29	0.79	1.59	3.29
Gas (1 gal.)	0.31	0.95	1.95	3.95
Record Album/CD	3.50	7.95	16.95	29.95
Movie Tickets	2.00	4.00	8.00	16.00

As you can see, we're now paying at least twice as much for bread, gasoline, and movie tickets as we did 20 years ago. If prices continue to go up in this fashion, 20 years from now we'll be paying the estimated prices shown above.

The unfortunate truth is that the cost of some things will go up much faster than your annual cost-of-living raise. As I said earlier, not only will you need enough money to retire comfortably, you'll need an investment program that generates inflation-proof income: income that either keeps up with or exceeds the rate of inflation. During the 20 or 30 years you spend in retirement, your expenses are going to increase.

The Biggest Risk

We all know someone who's lost money on a poorly perform-ing stock, a shaky real estate deal, or in the casinos of Las Vegas. As chancy as all these things are, there's only one that's more hazardous to your financial health, and that's not invest-ing—investing wisely, that is.

We've already seen how inflation (along with taxes, but we'll get to that later), is your money's biggest enemy. No mat-ter how much you earn, the rising cost of living is going to erode your purchasing power year after year. And the bottom-line truth is that most of us don't have unlimited earning potential. Whether you're an auto mechanic, a physician, or an executive vice president, you probably have an idea of how much you can expect to bring home every year...and can count on it being pretty much the same until the day you retire. Without the bonanza of a winning lottery ticket or inheriting your rich Aunt Minnie's entire estate, how are you ever going to have enough money set aside for the inevitable time when you can't or don't want to work anymore?

A Penny Saved is a Not a Penny Earned

A couple of generations ago financial planning was much easier. Putting aside 10% of your income in a savings account every month was considered basic common sense, and enough to cover whatever "rainy day" might arrive. But that was before a three-day hospital stay cost $30,000, and four-year college expenses hit six figures.

Even if you have the discipline to save every month (and studies show that Baby Boomers are saving less than the two generations before them), it will not provide the security you'll need in your later years. In fact, allowing your money to sit in a savings account for years is the equivalent of planting an orchid in the desert: it will not grow.

Let's assume you can manage to sock away $50,000 over the next 20 years: that's saving $2500 per year. At the current 3% interest rate for a passbook savings account, how much will you have in the bank 20 years from now?

The obvious answer—$50,000 plus the interest that's accrued over 20 years (in this case, $19,191)—isn't quite correct. To begin with, you must pay tax on the interest earned; if you're in the 28% tax bracket, the $19,191 you've earned in interest will be reduced by $5373, which lowers your interest earnings to $13,818.

Inflation, however, will do more damage to your savings than taxes. Inflation erodes the value of your money year after year. On the following page, the table "20 Years' Savings" shows what happens to your savings when you save at a low interest rate over a long term. In the top line, you'll see the deposited amount; the second shows the accrued 3% annual interest; the third, 28% tax on interest; the fourth, the negative effect of inflation—the amount that the *value* of your savings is reduced because of the rising cost of living. The final line, "Real Dollars Saved" shows what your savings will be worth in 20 years. In other words, in 20 years, your $50,000 plus interest will be worth only $30,874 in today's dollars.

20 YEARS' SAVINGS
($2500 per year, plus Interest, minus Tax & Inflation)

	Year 1	Year 5	Year 10	Year 15	Year 20
Amount Saved	$2500	$12,500	$25,000	$37,500	$50,000
+ 3% Interest (cumulative)	+$75	+$1171	+$4520	+$10,392	+$19,191
- 28% Tax (cumulative)	-$21	-$328	-$1266	-$2910	-$5373
- 5% Inflation (cumulative)	-$125	-$2007	-$7756	-$17,838	-$32,944
Real Dollars Saved	$2,429	$11,336	$20,498	$27,144	$30,874

When you discover what your money could have been doing for you during those 20 years, saving at 3% per annum is going to seem pretty foolish. Even so, some people have a hard time letting go of the savings mentality. Putting money in the bank makes them feel secure. After all, it's safe. Most people interpret this to mean risk-free, but they're wrong.

I'll say it again: the biggest risk you can take with your money is not investing it.

Imagine that inflation is a train moving along a track. To keep up, you've got to move ahead at the same speed. At 5% inflation, your salary must increase 5% per year; if you're just making ends meet now, your income will have to increase much more if you're going to save.

Just how fast is that train going, anyway?

Chances are it's moving ahead a lot faster than you are, and will be clear out of sight before you retire. It's not going to stop just because you stop working, either. The only hope you have of winning this race is to outrun the train—now and forever. And that means a long-term investment plan with an annual return greater than the rate of inflation. Or, even better, with an investment in real estate, you can allow inflation to work for you.

Worst-Case Scenarios

There are other reasons why an investment plan is crucial. To paraphrase a popular bumper sticker, "Stuff happens."

None of us is exempt from life's setbacks. Divorce, the death of a spouse, costly litigation, accidents, job loss or major illness can have a devastating effect on your finances. For the most part, we don't plan for these things, because we believe they only happen to other people. Solid financial planning will not only help protect your future, it will help protect your present lifestyle.

A Vision

The whole point of this chapter is to get you thinking about your future. No one likes to contemplate getting older, but I can assure you that it's much better to think about it now than later: ask anyone who's 65 or 70 and still working, or trying to get by on Social Security.

Let's take you, for instance. Let's say you're 45. Think fifteen years into the future. Now you're 60. For the generation that once believed in trusting no one over 30, this is harsh news. But believe me, unless things go really badly for you, you're going to get there.

When you're 60, would you like to be in the same financial position you're in now?

Probably not.

Close your eyes and think on this: What if, in fifteen years, you owned 10 houses in your home town free and clear? Let's say they're average homes, by today's prices: each worth $150,000. That means you'd have an estate worth $1.5 million. And that estate would be generating $100,000 in inflation-proof income every year.

Can you imagine how this would change your financial picture?

There's one little modification: your home town might not be the best place to purchase your 10 houses. So instead of owning 10 houses in your home town, you'll own 10 houses in the best markets in the U.S.

Impossible, you say.

But it isn't. It's much easier than you might think. Keep reading, and I'll show you how.

REPLAY

Everyone needs to plan for retirement.

You can't count on Social Security benefits alone.

People are retiring earlier, and living longer. You may need enough money to live on for 20, 30 or even 40 years.

3% inflation decreases your purchasing power by one-third in only 10 years.

The biggest risk you take with your money is not investing it.

Putting your money in a low-interest savings account for short-term goals is worthwhile, but when you save over the long term, you actually lose money.

Without financial planning, life's setbacks can devastate your finances.

2

WHY YOU SHOULD INVEST IN REAL ESTATE

As I said in the first chapter, this isn't just a book about real estate. It's a book about taking charge of your future, about doing something powerful with your money that can mean the difference between living the life of your dreams and retirement poverty. It's about financial planning (those dreaded words again). It just so happens that real estate is a great vehicle for meeting all of your financial needs.

Leverage, fixed-rate loans and tax deductions offer a package of benefits found in no other investment type. Historically, real estate values have increased at 1.5 times the rate of inflation; many individual markets have exceeded that figure. The escalating value of your investment home combined with a decreasing loan balance offers the opportunity to dramatically increase your net worth with a minimum investment.

Leverage

What, exactly, is leverage? It means that you're using a lever, just like when you use a lever to lift something heavy. In terms of money and investments, it means you're using other people's money; typically, a bank's money.

For example, if you buy a $100,000 house with a $10,000 down payment, that's 10 to 1 leverage: you're using a lever of $10,000 with a loan of $90,000 to raise $100,000.

Traditionally, only real estate can be leveraged to such a degree. In the stock market, the highest leverage you can get is 2 to 1 (and, occasionally, 3 to 1, on selected stocks). In other words, you may be able to buy stock for only 50% of its price, with the brokerage firm providing the other 50%. This is known as buying on margin. Buying on margin is very risky. If the stock dips below the price you paid for it, you may be forced to sell it—at the worst possible time—in what is known as a "margin call."

Conceivably, you can get leverage for any investment type, i.e., if your mother offers to lend you 90% of the funds to buy stock. But when you're applying to institutions for a loan, only real estate can be leveraged 10 to 1.

Leverage is one of the benefits to investing in real estate: you can buy a $100,000 home for only $10,000 down, or you can buy $1 million worth of real estate for only $100,000. It's one of the keys to building a financially secure future. There's a saying among real estate professionals, "What you owe today, you'll own tomorrow." Why? Because after your initial 10% investment, the tenant pays off the remainder of the mortgage for you.

The Miracle of the American Fixed-Rate Loan

Thanks to the post-World War II strategy that enabled people to buy homes easily, we have something in this country that exists in very few places in the world: the fixed-rate loan.

The fixed-rate loan is a bonanza. It's a gift. It's incredible.

I was born outside the U.S. When you come from another country, and you see what's available here, certain things stand out. A 30-year, fixed-rate mortgage is one of them. You may take it for granted, but foreigners don't.

Why is it so amazing? Let's take a look at the numbers:

When you take out a $90,000 30-year loan, say at an 8% fixed rate, your monthly payment of principal and interest is approximately $660 a month. You know for a fact that this is going to be the payment for the next 30 years—it will never change. Even if, in 20 years, $660 is barely enough to buy dinner for two, it will still be your mortgage payment.

When I speak in Europe, my audience invariably stops me when I tell them about fixed-rate loans. They think I don't have my facts straight. They think it's not possible. Or they think I'm just plain crazy. They can't comprehend how, in a country where the cost of living keeps rising, banks will lend money for 30 years where the principal and interest payment and the balance of the loan never change—except to go down.

For anyone from outside the U.S., this is truly an unbelievable thing. In other countries, loans are indexed to inflation. It's not inconceivable to get a loan for $100,000 where the initial payment is $700 a month, and 10 years later the payment is $5000 a month, and the balance of the loan is

$200,000. Why? Because the principal, interest and balance of the loan increase to keep up with inflation.

Fixed-rate loans are not just inflation-proof, they're inflation fighters.

We've already seen how the price of everything is steadily going up. Everything—except your mortgage balance. Which in fact is going down every month, along with your mortgage payment, which, because of inflation, is eroded—it gets smaller and smaller and smaller all the time.

By financing your investment with a fixed-rate loan, you're actually making money. It's as if, in 1980, you'd made a deal with Coca-Cola that you would never have to pay more than 25 cents for a single can of Coke...but only for the next thirty years; after that, it's free. Imagine that! In 1990, when everyone else was shelling out 65 cents, your deal looked pretty

---

PAUSE:

Throughout the book, I'll be talking about 30-year, fixed-rate loans, but it's important to keep one thing in mind: you don't have to pay off a 30-year loan in 30 years. You can pay it off whenever you want to—whatever works for your particular financial plan. You can also refinance the original loan to a 15-year note. The advantages of a 30-year loan are that it has lower monthly payments, and it's easier to qualify for it. As your investment home increases in value and rental prices rise, you can decide whether to put the profits "in your pocket" or use them to pay off the loan sooner.

good. Now, when a Coke might cost one dollar, it's even better. And 10 years hence, when your $1.50 Coke is absolutely free, it'll feel fabulous.

Real Estate Values

When you buy a $100,000 property with only 10% down, and you finance the $90,000 balance with a 30-year, fixed-rate loan, you've done something very powerful for your future.

Why? Because over the long-term—which I define as a minimum of five years, and preferably ten—hard assets, such as real estate, will *on average* rise in value with the cost of living.

For example, let's say you bought a $100,000 home in an average market, where the property values don't really go up, but just keep pace with inflation. This is called zero appreciation; however, the value of the home is still increasing 3% per year because of inflation.

After one year, your $100,000 home will be worth $103,000. When you put only $10,000 down, that's a 30% return on your investment.

You think that's an imaginary figure? Not at all! Overall, home values appreciate at 1.5 times the rate of inflation, which would bump that $3000 profit up to $4500. And good real estate markets consistently surpass the average.

I began investing in Las Vegas in the mid-1980s. From 1987, when I stopped buying there, to 1990, only three years later, the market had risen so rapidly that I made an 800% return on my investments.

Whether you make a 30% return in one year or an 800%

return in three years, investing in real estate and holding it for the long term will enable your money to grow at a rate that will consistently outstrip inflation. To go back to the train metaphor from Chapter One, once you invest in real estate, you're already staying ahead of the train. And in a good market—it doesn't have to be booming, mind you, just going up at a steady pace—you're going to quickly leave that train in the dust.

But that isn't the only benefit. There's more good news to come.

Financing College Expenses or Retirement

There are two financial planning dilemmas that I hear most often. In the first, Tom and Jenny, a young couple in their 20s, want to send their newborn daughter to college in 18 years. They know that college is already incredibly expensive; they can't even begin to predict what it's going to cost in 18 years. They only know that they can't afford it now, and they don't know how they'll be able to afford it later.

In the second, Marion and Paul, in their 40s, would like to retire in 20 years. They have a 401(k) and an IRA but, even so, they can see that another 20 years of contributions and compounding isn't going to provide them with the kind of wealth they'd like to have. Like most Baby Boomers, they don't envision spending their retirement camped out on the couch in front of the boob tube. They want to travel, play golf and tennis, and set up a trust fund for their kids. What can they do to ensure that their retirement lifestyle will be all that they desire?

A Simple Method

Many people get confused when trying to see 15 or 20 years into the future. Even when you know exactly what you want (and most of us don't; we only know that we want to have enough to maintain our present standard of living), trying to estimate expenses, future financial goals and prepare for the unexpected is simply mind-boggling. Who really knows what the next 20 years will bring, or exactly how much money will be necessary to live comfortably two decades hence?

You might think you need a crystal ball: one that will calculate future earnings, taxes and inflation, and provide a clear vision of what your life will look like 20 years from now.

Happily, a crystal ball isn't required. You don't have to see 20 years into the future. You can estimate your future needs by thinking in today's dollars. The two examples below will show you how it's done.

Using Real Estate as a College Fund

Let's start with Tom and Jenny, who wanted to plan for their daughter's college education.

First, what's the cost of a four-year university today? Current estimates place the combined costs of tuition, housing and expenses at an average of $80,000.

What Tom and Jenny needed was an investment that was inflation-proof; in other words, one that would increase in value along with the rising costs of a college education.

I suggested that they buy a $100,000 home with $10,000 down, and finance the remaining $90,000 with a 30-year, fixed rate loan. However, there's no rule that says you have to take 30 years to pay off a 30-year mortgage. Instead of 30 years, I recommended that they pay off the loan in 18 years.

How? By making an extra payment on the principal every year. After a few years, their tenants' rent is likely to rise with the cost of living, but their mortgage payment will remain the same. The rental income will make the extra principal payment for them. After a few more years, the rents are still likely to be rising—so not only is the house making the extra principal payment, it's also paying them. For most of those 18 years, the house will be generating profits. After 18 years go by, they'll have a free and clear $100,000 (in today's dollars) home that will cover the cost of their daughter's $80,000 (in today's dollars) education. Both the home and the college expenses should keep up with the cost of living in a similar manner. There's plenty of extra here to sell the house or to refinance it, and still come out ahead.

"And if you want to send your daughter to Harvard with a Porsche," I added, "buy two houses."

Using Real Estate for Retirement Income

How about Marion and Paul, who wanted to retire in 20 years?

I asked them to estimate the annual income they'd need if they were to retire today. How much would it take for them to live the life of their dreams—now?

They replied that $50,000 per year would cover all of their living expenses and financial goals: travel, trust fund, etc. What Marion and Paul needed was an income that was inflation-proof—one that would continue to generate the equiva-

RENTAL PROPERTY
As COLLEGE FUND

	Year 1	Year 5	Year 10	Year 15	Year 18
Rental Income	$12,000	$14,586	$18,616	$23,758	$27,504
PI + $1500 Extra Principal	$9420	$9420	$9420	$9420	$9420
Tax & Insurance	$2232*	$1654	$2111	$2694	$3119
Annual Profit	$348	$3512	$7085	$11,644	$14,965
Property Value	$105,000	$127,630	$162,890	$207,890	$240,660
Mortgage Balance	$87,664	$78,920	$59,717	$31,108	$0
Equity	$17,336	$48,710	$103,173	$176,783	$240,660

*Private Mortgage Insurance (PMI) is estimated at $936 annually. On investment homes, PMI is cancelled when equity increases to 25% (20% on owner-occupied homes).

PMI has been added to first-year figures. The increase in Rental Income, Tax & Insurance, and Property Value has been calculated using a 5% annual inflation rate. PI = Principal & Interest.

lent of $50,000 in today's dollars year after year...even 20 or 30 or 40 years from now.

Suppose, like Tom and Jenny, they bought a $100,000 home with $10,000 down, and paid off the loan in 20 years. Now it's free and clear, with no mortgage to pay. There are, however, certain expenses that will continue: property tax, insurance, property management, vacancies and repairs. I can tell you from my vast experience of buying thousands of homes that these expenses are going to run approximately $400 a month.

Now, what's the monthly rent on a $100,000 home? Where I live, in the San Francisco Bay Area, it can be as little as $600 or $700, which is why I don't invest there. But there are numerous markets in the U.S. where a $100,000 home rents for approximately $1000 a month. To name just a few: Phoenix, Arizona; Orlando, Jacksonville and Tampa, Florida; and Las Vegas, Nevada.

If Marion and Paul's house is renting for $1000 each month, and their expenses are $400 each month, that's a $600 profit per month. If one house brings in $600 per month, how many houses will they need to make $4200 per month, or $50,000 per year?

Seven houses.

One is Not Enough

Does buying seven houses seem like a far-fetched notion? If you think it is, you're in the majority. Most of us are brought up with a singular goal: to buy our own home. The home you own and live in is probably your biggest asset, yet most of us don't think past our first home purchase, unless it's to trade up to a larger, more expensive house.

A few months ago I was in New York, on my way to give a lecture for the Learning Annex. The cab driver, a friendly fellow in his fifties, asked what I would be lecturing on. When I said real estate, he told me about his house in upstate New York. He'd bought it 25 years ago, for only $20,000. It was

RETIREMENT INCOME
from RENTAL PROPERTY

	Total Income (mo.)	Total Expense (mo.)	Total Profit (mo.)	Total Profit (annual)
1 Rental Property	$1000	$400	$600	$7200
2 Rental Properties	$2000	$800	$1200	$14,400
3 Rental Properties	$3000	$1200	$1800	$21,600
4 Rental Properties	$4000	$1600	$2400	$28,800
5 Rental Properties	$5000	$2000	$3000	$36,000
6 Rental Properties	$6000	$2400	$3600	$43,200
7 Rental Properties	$7000	$2800	$4200	$50,400

now worth over $525,000. He was proud of his investment, for good reason. But I couldn't help thinking what I always think when I hear stories like this (and I hear many), "Why didn't he buy two houses? Or three? He'd be a millionaire now, and wouldn't have to drive a cab!"

I know that buying even one investment home requires a kind of quantum jump in the way you think about yourself and your future. But to buy seven, or 10, or 15 homes? Only the most experienced real estate investors would do that, right?

Wrong.

Ask any one of the hundreds of people—busy people, just

like you—whom I've worked with over the past 15 years. None of them are experts, and yet many of them have purchased five, 10, 15, or 20 homes or more. The only difference between you and them is that their financial future is secure. It's a done deal. They don't have to worry about it anymore.

PAUSE:

It isn't necessary to buy all your investment homes at once, of course. You can build your portfolio over time (see Chapter 12 for examples). The main thing is to begin thinking beyond the limited notion that "one is enough," or that "bigger is better."

Investing for the Shorter Term

This is all great, you're thinking, if I wanted to retire in 15 or 20 years, but I'm 55 and I'd like to retire in 10!

What should you do if you've got less time to plan?

To gain the benefits of your investment sooner, you need to use less leverage when buying properties. Putting a down payment of 20%, 30% or 40% will mean a smaller mortgage. The rental income from the property will generate profits immediately—profits you can then use to pay off the mortgage in ten years.

For an in-depth scenario of a shorter-term investment, see Chapter 12.

Back to Marion and Paul

For the couple who wanted to retire in 20 years, I recommended buying seven homes. If the homes average $100,000 each, they would need approximately $80,000 in down payments and closing costs. I'm not implying in any way that $80,000 is small change; there's no question that it's a lot of money. But look at what it will buy:

- $700,000 in real property
- Profits "in your pocket" within 5 to 10 years
- $50,000 a year in inflation-proof retirement income
- A net worth of $700,000, in today's dollars

Now, that's a very solid financial future, but this is only the tip of the iceberg. In addition to providing you with profits, inflation-proof investments and income, and greatly increased net worth, your real estate investments can do something very, very special for you that no other investment type can—something you'll appreciate every time April 15th comes around.

Tax Benefits for Real Estate Investors

In the above examples, I haven't factored in the tax deductions you can take as a real estate investor, which would make the outcome considerably rosier. Most people are aware of the tax breaks that homeowners enjoy, but few know that investors profit from an even greater number of deductions. If leverage and the 30-year, fixed-rate loan can be considered gifts, then the tax benefits are like a whole bundle from Santa. (For a complete analysis of tax issues, see Chapter 14.)

Just as they are on an owner-occupied home, mortgage interest and real estate taxes are deductible on investment properties. In addition, all repairs are deductible, as are all expenses associated with the property, such as travel and lodging, telephone, and tax preparation.

But this isn't all.

Unlike the home you own and live in, you can depreciate investment property. This is a just-for-tax-purposes, imaginary loss that's calculated over 27.5 years. On a $100,000 property, the tax deduction is approximately $3600 per year. If your adjusted gross income is less than $100,000 per year, you can claim up to $25,000 in these passive losses.

This is the second bit of news that astounds my European audiences.

"You mean to tell me," they say incredulously, "that in the U.S., you can get a fixed-rate loan for 30 years on a piece of property that's going to rise in value, and you can pretend that this same piece of property is declining in value and get a tax break? What kind of country is this?"

You know what I say in reply?

"It's a great country."

When we add tax benefits to the above estimate of what your $80,000 investment will bring, it becomes even more extraordinary:

- $700,000 in real property
- Profits "in your pocket" within 5 to 10 years
- $50,000 a year in inflation-proof retirement income
- $25,000 each year in tax deductible depreciation
- A net worth of $700,000, in today's dollars—imagine what your net worth will be in 20 years!

One Last Thing: What About the Stock Market?

Personally, I have nothing against the stock market. Done wisely, it's also a good way to invest, and a well-rounded investment portfolio will include, at the very least, some mutual funds. Over the long term, the stock market also keeps up with or outstrips inflation. But real estate is by its very nature a more stable investment.

The stock market has made countless people some serious profit, but these profits are precarious and can be lost just as easily as they come. In one year, from January to December 2000, the NASDAQ fell 40%! Thousands of stock market investors have been devastated by the market's decline. Some of you may remember a recent headline: "The Man Who Lost $6 Billion in One Day." This reflects the transient nature of the stock market "quick gain." The smart stock investor comes to me, wanting to convert some of his unstable stock gains into a stable real estate portfolio.

Another difference between investing in stocks and real estate is the opportunity to use 10 to 1 leverage when buying property. If you buy $10,000 worth of stock without buying on margin (most people don't buy on margin, because it's dangerous), and it goes up 3%, you make $300. If you buy a $100,000 home with $10,000 down, and it goes up 3%, you make $3000. This leverage will work against you if property values go down, but the whole premise of this book is that you hold your real estate investments for the long term—and in the long term, real estate values have on average risen 1.5 times the rate of inflation.

REPLAY

Leverage offers the ability to dramatically increase your net worth with a minimum investment.

A 30-year, fixed-rate loan actually makes money for you.

You can tailor a 30-year loan to meet your financial planning goals by paying it off sooner, in the number of years that you choose.

Real estate overall appreciates at 1.5 times the rate of inflation.

Use real estate as an inflation-proof investment for financial goals, and as inflation-proof income for retirement.

Your own home is probably your greatest asset. Remember you can substantially increase your net worth just by buying one more home!

Think beyond your first purchase: 5, 10 and even 20 homes are within your reach.

You can build your portfolio over time.

Tax benefits for real estate investors exceed the tax benefits offered to homeowners.

3

SHORT TERM VS. LONG TERM INVESTING

ANY TIME YOU INVEST IN REAL ESTATE FOR THE SHORT-TERM (which I define as five years or less), you take a big risk with your money.

While it's true there's money to be made buying, renovating and selling bargain properties, it's a challenging and time-consuming endeavor, one that's best left to full-time real estate experts. Even though real estate outstrips inflation over the long-term, in the short-term, markets will fluctuate. If you purchase an investment property intending to make a profit in less than five years, you're going to be at the mercy of the market—and it has no mercy.

Some people spend an inordinate amount of time charting the ups and downs of real estate markets, hoping to catch a "wave" that will enable them to buy low and sell high. But this is something that no one can predict with total accuracy. The exclusion of just one important factor can send the whole forecast crashing down like a house of cards. How many "seers" foresaw the 1994 debacle in Orange County, California, when one of the most affluent counties in the country declared bankruptcy and sent home prices spiraling downward?

Happily for busy investors, building wealth with real estate is not contingent upon catching one wave. You don't need to spend your time charting the fluctuations of the market. It's much better—and more lucrative in the long run—to ride the waves and let them take you safely to the farther shore.

A Long and Short-Term Story

Earlier, I told you about my experience when I began working and how I wanted more to show for my hard work after 15 years than my colleagues did. Since I grew up in a family of real estate developers, I knew something about real estate. And being very aware of the advantages of investing in real estate in the U.S., real estate simply made a lot of sense to me.

At first, I started looking around the Bay Area. At the time, 1983 and '84, it was possible to buy a decent home in Palo Alto (where Stanford University and Hewlett-Packard are located), for $150,000. These days that seems like an imaginary figure, because the current median home price in Palo Alto is around $600,000. Even then, however, that $150,000 house couldn't rent for more than about $700 a month: the discrepancy between the rental income and the mortgage payment was too great. Instead of buying a house in Palo Alto, I bought a house in Sunnyvale and a small apartment building in San Jose. As I looked around for more properties to buy, I realized that if I wanted to keep on investing and make a difference in my future, I couldn't do it in the Bay Area; rents were too low in proportion to the monthly payments.

About a year later, I started buying single family homes in Las Vegas, Nevada. Las Vegas at that time was a depressed real estate market, and the houses cost about $40,000 each. I went about it very aggressively. In my first year and a half, I bought 22 houses.

Many of my engineer friends at Hewlett-Packard, who were logical people, were impressed by what I was doing. Very soon I was leading a group of 20 friends, all of whom bought investment homes in Las Vegas. We kept on buying there until mid-1987, when the Las Vegas market went up dramatically. The increase in prices was a big bonus for the homes we had already bought, but it wasn't a good time to buy more.

We held on to what we had bought in Las Vegas and started buying in Portland, Oregon. At the time, Portland was a slow real estate market and we bought single family homes inexpensively, until Portland, too, started going up.

In 1987, California home prices began to rise rapidly. People were making money hand over fist. As I read the Sunday paper each week, I was astounded by what was happening: price increases of 30% and 35% a year were not uncommon. I owned only a couple of properties in California, so I wasn't benefiting much from the booming market. I decided to stop investing elsewhere and buy houses in the Bay Area, to take advantage of the market's sudden upswing.

I chose to buy in Santa Rosa, 60 miles north of San Francisco. At the time, it was fairly inexpensive. I began by buying four houses, each for $110,000. I financed them with

10% down, for a total of $11,000 down each and the closing costs. Indeed, they went up to almost $180,000 about a year and a half later, which was an excellent return on my investment.

When I was ready to buy my fifth house, the realtors I worked with connected me with a developer in Santa Rosa who had just finished building an entire sub-division. He had a whole street of unsold homes; he needed to sell and sell fast. So I offered to buy the entire street, and I got a discount, since I was buying in bulk. The average price per home was $99,000. I sold the whole street within ten months, for an average price of $142,000 per home, which means I made a net profit of approximately $30,000 on each.

By the end of 1989, I needed a rest. I decided to go to Hawaii for a whole week, and do absolutely nothing except lay on the beach.

Which I proceeded to do quite successfully for about three days. On the fourth day, I found myself in a car with a realtor, looking at houses on Maui. Hawaii, at the time, was a booming market. In Tokyo, you could borrow money very cheaply, almost free, and many people from Japan would come and buy properties for cash—in Hawaii especially and on the mainland as well.

So I called my friends in the Bay Area and said, "I've just seen a new condo development that I think would be a great investment. There are sixteen units left in phase one, and I think we should buy them all. I think we can sell them quickly to Japanese buyers for cash."

And they said, "We really like your track record and your

judgement, but this is the first time you've ever been to Maui, so no thanks."

So I bought whatever I could buy as an individual. When you're from the mainland, and you're buying in Hawaii with financing from a Hawaiian lender, and you own more than 10 properties, which were all true in my case, you really have to put a lot of cash down. So I only bought two: one for $305,000, and a second for $250,000. I hired a designer to furnish them for $23,000 apiece. The first I sold in six weeks for $425,000, and the second went for $394,000 two months later.

It's very nice to go to Hawaii on vacation and make this kind of profit, but since then when I want to rest I go to Mexico, where it's harder to pull off deals like this.

As in Comedy, Timing is Everything

Why am I telling you all this? Three main reasons: first, I want to give you some background; second, I want to brag, and third, it illustrates the difference between short-term and long-term investment.

I've described two types of buying real estate so far. In the first, I bought homes in Las Vegas and other markets as rental properties to be held long-term. In the second, I purchased an entire street and sold it quickly, then "flipped" condos in Maui, and made large profits in a few months. Clearly, the second type of buying sounds a lot more exciting. Who wouldn't want to come back from a vacation a couple of hundred thousand dollars richer?

But when you look at those short-term deals more carefully, you'll see that they could have turned out quite differently. When I tell you the story of the condos in Maui, or of the street in Santa Rosa, they sound perfect. They are perfect, because they're finished. But suppose that I was speaking to you right now and said, "You know, I was just in Maui last week, and there are condos, we should buy them, come on, let's go, let's do it."

You'd say, "Hold on a minute. How can you be sure that you can sell them quickly for a profit?" You'd be absolutely right to be so cautious. More than anything else, it was luck and timing that made those deals happen.

I closed escrow on the Hawaiian condos in January 1989. The first one sold in April 1989, and the second one in June, two months later. Guess what? In the summer of 1989, the Hawaiian real estate market tumbled—absolutely crashed.

If I had taken my vacation a little bit later, or if the condos hadn't sold so soon, I would have been stuck with two vacation rentals, with a lot of my cash tied up in them and a negative cash flow. The Hawaiian market went down so much that the condos' value was soon less than the loans I had taken out.

I was lucky. What about the street in Santa Rosa that I bought and sold? Same thing. I started buying in Santa Rosa in January of 1988. By the time I purchased the street it was mid-1988. I closed escrow in July, which means I finished selling the street just about May of 1989.

In May of 1989, the California market started to slow down. If the deal in Santa Rosa had closed a few months later than it did, I would've lost a lot of money and been stuck with a whole street of homes that were declining in value.

As it stood I made a lot of money on both of those deals, but it was nothing but luck and timing. And that's always the case. Whenever you want to speculate and make a quick buck in real estate, you're taking a risk. You're hoping it will happen, but you had better be financially prepared to hold on to the property for the long-term, just in case.

The Four Conditions of Flipping Properties

"Flipping" a property means selling it soon after you purchase it. The intention, of course, is to make a quick profit.

As I said earlier, quick profits in real estate rely too much on luck and timing to be a dependable source of income. It's not investing, it's gambling.

The real estate "gurus" who extol the virtues of flipping properties make it sound simple; too simple, in fact. According to them, anyone can find a bargain property and sell it quickly for a profit. This strategy sounds reasonable, but when you examine it more carefully, you discover it's as full of holes as a slice of Swiss cheese. To successfully flip a property, four essential conditions are required: you must buy below market value; the market must keep rising; you must find a buyer who will pay full price; and your profits must exceed your actual costs. Let's look at these elements one at a time:

You've just purchased a bargain property.

What exactly makes a property a "bargain"? By definition, a bargain property has an appraised or estimated value above what you paid for it, i.e., a single family home appraised at

$100,000 that you purchase for $80,000. The catch is this: if no one is offering to pay $100,000, then the property is not actually worth $100,000. (And if they are, your $80,000 bid will be ignored.)

No matter what the appraised or estimated value of a property, its actual worth is based on what the seller can get for it. If you purchase a "$100,000 property" for $80,000, you've just bought a property worth—guess what?—$80,000.

The market will keep rising in the short term.

As illustrated above, even booming markets can suddenly stop booming, and even plummet. If short-term market fluctuations were predictable, then few people would ever lose money on real estate.

But markets are not entirely predictable in the short term. In order to sell your property quickly for a profit, the market must rise.

You'll find a buyer who will pay full price.

If you weren't willing to pay more than $80,000 for the property, how can you be certain that, in a month or two, you'll find a buyer willing to pay $100,000 or more?

If the market is rising very rapidly, this may happen. Otherwise, you're relying on the "bigger fool" theory: that someone with limited knowledge of local real estate values will pay an inflated price for your property.

Profits will exceed your actual costs.

Let's assume that you were able to sell your $80,000 property in three months for $100,000. How much money have you made?

First, you have to deduct the down payment (10%, or $8,000); closing costs and lender's fees for a $72,000 loan; realtor commissions when you sell; mortgage payments until the property sells (let's assume you can sell it in three months, a fairly quick turn-around); and any costs associated with repairing and showing the property. (Let's suppose that it isn't a fixer-upper, but just needed some cleaning up and a bit of landscaping.) And, of course, you have to pay taxes on your profits. So what's the bottom line?

Gross profit:	$20,000	
Closing costs on purchase:		($2,000)
Commissions on sale:		($6,000)
Mortgage payments:		($1,800)
Painting, cleaning, repairs, landscaping:		($2,000)
Misc. expenses:		($1,000)
NET PROFIT:	$7200	
Less Federal income tax (28% tax bracket)		($2,016)
AFTER TAX PROFIT:	$5184	

In my opinion, that isn't much to show for the time, money and effort involved in finding a "bargain" property, making cosmetic improvements, and putting it back on the market. And yet, the selling price of $100,000 represents a 25% increase over the purchase price of $80,000—an enormous jump for only three months.

Long-Term Investing

As illustrated by the chart opposite, real estate really shows its power over the long term. The figures in the chart represent an investment in a $100,000 property, with a 10% down payment and the remaining $90,000 financed with an 8% mortgage.

Line one shows rental income starting at $12,000 per year, and rising 5% per year. Line two shows how principal and interest payments remain the same. Line three shows a 5% rise in tax and insurance each year (these figures are based on property tax rates for the state of Arizona; some states may be lower or higher). First year insurance figures are higher because of private mortgage insurance, or PMI, estimated at $936 annually for a $90,000 mortgage. PMI can be cancelled as soon as you have 25% equity in the property (this applies to investment properties; you need only 20% equity in owner-occupied properties to cancel PMI).

The fourth and fifth lines of the chart reveal how profits and property values become very powerful over the long term.

Most importantly, the mortgage balance decreases as rental income and property value rise. I've calculated the increase in property value at 5% per year—a conservative figure for many markets. And yet you can see that with only a $10,000 investment, in 20 years this property will be generating over $18,000 per year in profit, and have a value of nearly a quarter million dollars!

LONG TERM INVESTMENT PROFITS

	Year 1	Year 5	Year 10	Year 15	Year 20
Rental Income	$12,000	$14,586	$18,616	$23,758	$30,324
Principal & Interest	$7920	$7920	$7920	$7920	$7920
Tax & Insurance	$2232*	$1654	$2111	$2694	$3439
Annual Profit	$1848	$5012	$8585	$13,144	$18,965
Property Value	$105,000	$127,630	$162,890	$207,890	$240,660
Mortgage Balance	$89,280	$85,590	$78,930	$69,120	$54,450
Equity	$15,720	$42,040	$83,960	$138,770	$186,210

*Private Mortgage Insurance (PMI) is estimated at $936 annually. On investment homes, PMI is cancelled when equity increases to 25% (20% on owner-occupied homes).

PMI has been added to first-year figures. The increase in Rental Income, Tax & Insurance, and Property Value has been calculated using a 5% annual inflation rate.

REPLAY

Properly buying, renovating and selling properties is usually a full-time job done by professionals.

In the short term, markets fluctuate. Over the long term, they steadily go up, rising on average 1.5 times the cost of living.

You don't have to chart the markets, just stay in for the long term.

Short-term profits rely on luck and timing.

Even if you speculate, you must be prepared to hold on to the property for the long term.

Real estate really shows its power over the long term.

4

WHAT TO BUY

MOST REAL ESTATE BOOKS PRESENT AN OVERVIEW OF THE types of real estate in which you can invest, from small apartment buildings and condos to commercial real estate and undeveloped land. I'm not going to do that. I've tried just about every kind of real estate investment there is, and there's only one that works for the busy investor: the single family home.

A True American Dream

Single family homes are the stuff of which the American Dream is made. Everyone wants the picket fence, the yard, and the two-car garage. More than any other type of real estate, single family homes are always in demand, and are therefore the most liquid. When the market goes up, single family homes go up first and most. When the market goes down, single family homes go down last and least. As an investment, they're the most stable; as a piece of property, they're the easiest to rent, maintain, manage and sell. For busy investors, quality single family homes located in good neighborhoods offer the most effortless, stress-free real estate investment possible, with the best appreciation potential.

Single family homes are the best investment in terms of liquidity, financing, ease of management and appreciation. From experience, I know that single family homes are the safest, easiest and most dependable real estate investment you can make. Single family homes generate the financial benefits that will secure your future without the hassles that many other types of property entail. However, I stress that the only kind of single family homes to buy are quality single family homes, located in good neighborhoods.

What do I mean by "quality" single family homes?

I mean a house that's reasonably new, and in good structural condition. One that's aesthetically appealing, has a well-tended, functional yard, a garage, two baths, and at least three bedrooms. It doesn't have to be a showplace or the house of your dreams—in fact, it probably shouldn't be. But it should be a place where a family can live comfortably.

Don't Confuse Cash-Flow with Quality

If quality single family homes are such a great investment, you may be wondering, why haven't the other books you've read told you the same thing?

For one, buying a single family home isn't the most exciting investment. It doesn't have the same caché as, for instance, purchasing an apartment complex or a mini-mall. But along

PAUSE: The Top Six Reasons to Buy Single Family Homes

Financing is best for single family homes.

Single family homes typically appreciate faster than any other type of real estate, and maintain value better than any other type of real estate.

Single family homes are easiest to rent, manage, maintain and sell.

Single family homes attract stable tenants.

Single family homes are more liquid than other types of real estate.

Single family homes are most appropriate for "real people" (not just multi-millionaires).

with bragging rights go a lot of headaches. I've tried those other kinds of investments, yet I've made the most (and easiest) money with single family homes, the least "macho" real estate.

Do I care? Not at all.

Another reason is that quality single family homes often have the worst cash flow—at first glance. When you look at older, lower-quality single family homes in older, lower-quality neighborhoods, their cash flow seems better: a $50,000 house that rents for $700 is more profitable than a $100,000 house that rents for $1000. So why do I continue to recommend quality single family homes?

Because cash flow on paper doesn't tell the whole story. Older, low-quality properties require more repairs, and often the tenant turn-over is more frequent. These things not only cost you money, but time. In addition, a low-quality home won't appreciate as rapidly as a high-quality home.

Quality single family homes attract good, stable tenants who pay their rent on time and don't damage your property— and that's what's going to help make your investment work. Remember, you're investing for the long-term. A quality single family home will continue to rise in value, and your rental income will increase with the cost of living.

When you look at the big picture, you'll see that even a property that starts out with a negative cash flow can soon become positive. And you can't talk about cash flow without talking about cash flow after taxes. This is one time that Uncle Sam is giving money to you.

$100,000 SINGLE FAMILY HOME 5-YEAR CASH FLOW FIGURES

	Year 1	Year 2	Year 3	Year 4	Year 5
Rental Income	$12,000	$12,600	$13,230	$13,891	$14,586
Principal & Interest	$7920	$7920	$7920	$7920	$7920
Tax & Insurance	$3000	$3150	$3308	$3473	$3647
PMI + Expenses	$1236	$1236	$1236	$300	$300
Gross Profit <Loss>	<$156>	$294	$766	$2198	$2719
Depreciation Deduction	$3600	$3600	$3600	$3600	$3600
Tax Savings (28% bracket)	$1052	$926	$794	$393	$247
Net Profit	$896	$1220	$1560	$2591	$2966

*Private Mortgage Insurance (PMI) is estimated at $936 annually. On investment homes, PMI is cancelled when equity increases to 25% (20% on owner-occupied homes).

In the example shown above, first year figures show a before-tax loss, or negative cash flow, of $156. After adding in tax savings from the depreciation deduction, however, the property shows a net profit of $896. Each year, as rental rates increase, positive cash flow also increases, rising substantially in year four, after PMI is cancelled.

The Hidden Costs of Small Apartment Buildings

Of course, there are other types of real estate you can invest in which can work successfully—for example, large apartment complexes of over 100 units, or shopping malls. But by virtue of their cost, these kinds of real estate investments are available only to the very rich, or to syndications and corporations, etc.—not to the average person.

You may have read books that suggest buying a small apartment building—say four to ten units—as your first investment. The authors' main reason for this is that apartment buildings can generate positive cash flow.

It's often true that, on paper, small apartment buildings can seem like a dream come true. In reality, they can be a nightmare. The same authors who tell you to buy apartments will also tell you that managing them is a piece of cake, and that dealing with numerous tenants, repairs, etc., is a small price to pay for the all-important cash flow. But I can tell you that this isn't so: managing apartment buildings is more demanding than managing single family homes. For the busy investor who wants to have a life outside of real estate, small apartment buildings can be a sure path to ulcers and migraines...even bankruptcy and divorce.

To illustrate, let me tell you a story about a four-plex I bought in Albuquerque, New Mexico. Here's what it looked like on paper:

FOUR-PLEX CASH FLOW FIGURES

Purchase Price:	$27,000
10% Down:	$2,700
Mortgage:	$24,300
PITI:	$400 per month
Rental Income:	$1200 per month
Gross Profit:	$800 per month

It seems like an excellent deal, yes? Unfortunately, no. Here's what happened in real life:

I bought the four-plex in foreclosure from the government for only $2,700 down. Each unit rented for $300 a month. That's a $1200 monthly income against a $400 per month PITI (principal, interest, taxes and insurance). With an $800 per month profit, you would think that this was a good deal.

But the four-plex never had a positive cash-flow. There were many four-plexes in the area, so often at least one of the units in my four-plex was vacant. A number of tenants didn't pay rent, or damaged the property. It was constantly being repaired. I sold it for less than what I had paid for it, and felt lucky to get out before it ate up more of my cash.

Small apartment buildings can have "hidden" costs that don't show up in the initial numbers. Not to mention the price you pay with your sanity.

I'll repeat: don't confuse cash flow with quality. Remember, you're investing for the long-term.

The Truth About Foreclosures

Bargain properties, such as foreclosures, are the classic real estate lure. Now, I like a sale as much as the next guy. Who wouldn't want to buy a $100,000 house for only $60,000? That sounds great! Go to a couple of popular real estate seminars and you'll see foreclosure fever in action. Instant wealth! Overnight success! And where's it all come from? Foreclosures!

Listen long enough, and you'll get the impression that buying foreclosures is as easy as plucking ripe berries from a vine. But if you dive into the foreclosure field's thorny brambles, you may find that instead of plucking, you're the one who's getting…plucked.

You have to think logically. There are many people out there who specialize in foreclosure deals. A good number of them are making a living at it, and some of them are doing very well. However, these people are professionals who buy foreclosures full-time. Now, suppose they work in the same town where you're trying to buy foreclosures. Doesn't it stand to reason that if there's a good deal out there, they'll get to it long before you do? Of course they will! So what's left over for you, the busy, part-time investor?

I can tell you what's left over: the junk no one else wants.

You have to be really careful. It's too easy for more experienced people to manipulate and sway you. For instance, a seller could have a lousy property that he's dying to get rid of, but he's not giving it back to the bank or walking away from it because he doesn't want to ruin his credit. But he could lure you, the unsuspecting investor who just bought a home-study course on buying foreclosures, with his "bargain" price and his offer to give you $3000 at the close of escrow. And you think, "Wow! These tapes work!"

You know what the seller thinks? "What a sucker! I've been trying to get this white elephant off my hands for two years!"

The pros are always going to beat you to the best stuff. You'll get the leftovers. Even for the leftovers, you'll be competing with lots of other people who are looking for foreclosures part-time. And if you do this part-time, you could run great risks.

Even when a foreclosure deal appears to be easy and readily available, it may not be your best bet. I know this from experience. I have purchased dozens of VA (Veterans Administration) repossessed properties (repos) in various states. On the surface, these REOs (REO stands for "Real Estate Owned" and is the term commonly used when a lending institution forecloses on a property) seemed like great deals. Typically, they were sold by the VA for no money down or an extremely low down payment, such as $1,000. In the case of the no-money-down sales, the VA itself gave the buyer a 100% loan on the property—a 30-year, fixed rate loan at very attractive rates.

What could be more perfect, right? After analyzing what I had bought, however, I realized that buying beautiful, brand new homes at market value from a builder was a much better deal.

Here's why: the great financing and no-money-down terms were so enticing, many buyers greatly overbid the properties so that many sold at well over market value—not a great start! (Buyers submitted their bids for the REOs in sealed envelopes and the highest bidder "won.") The VA charged 2 loan points (2% of the loan); along with the other closing expenses, the total cost for the purchase was about 4% of the property value.

In addition, the REOs were sold in an as-is condition, and many of them had been vacant and boarded up for months prior to the sale. It took, on average, about 6% of the property's price to fix it up and bring it up to rental standard. The REOs also sold with the utilities turned off, and they could not be turned on until after the sale had taken place. In some cases, there were nasty surprises regarding the plumbing or electrical systems. Repairing those systems cost, on average, another 1.5% of the property price.

All in all, this "no-money-down" REO deal had an average cost of 10% to 11.5% of the property's price—and that's to buy an older, overpriced property in a neighborhood that, more often than not, the buyer didn't choose (and often wasn't a good neighborhood).

If, instead, I had bought a brand new property at market value, in a great part of town, the initial costs would have been about the same, the price in many cases would have been better, and usually the condition of the property as well as the neighborhood would have been infinitely better.

All in all, the brand new home would have made a far better real estate deal—and with no effort at all! The inferior REO deal required hunting, bidding, and repairing—lots of work—for a worse deal!

Unless you're a real estate expert, foreclosures can waste a lot of your time and money—but the whole point of *Remote Controlled Real Estate Riches* is that you don't need to be an expert to make great real estate investments.

After all, wouldn't you rather be playing golf than looking for termites?

Beware of the Motivated Seller

What does it mean when a seller is "motivated"? It means that he has a house he can't get rid of, or that he needs to sell so quickly he's willing to discount the price, or offer concessions.

In some instances, the motivated seller may loan you the down payment, and carry back a second mortgage. This can help you purchase a home, I'll admit. But do you have the time to look for these motivated sellers? For busy investors, motivated sellers are even harder to find than fast profits from foreclosures.

Too often, the truth behind the motivated seller is that the property is not a good investment. If it wasn't a good investment for him, it probably won't be for you. Implicit in this whole arrangement is that you're buying a bad property. Because if it wasn't a bad property, someone else would buy it for the full price and the seller wouldn't be "motivated" to make all those concessions.

Quality properties in good markets don't have motivated sellers. And I only recommend buying in good markets. What are good markets? That's the subject of the next chapter.

REPLAY

Single family homes are the best investment for the individual investor in terms of
- liquidity,
- financing,
- ease of management and
- appreciation.

Quality single family homes are best for long-term investments.

Don't confuse cash flow with quality.

A property that starts out with a negative cash flow can soon become positive.

Remember to include tax benefits into cash flow figures.

Small apartment buildings can have hidden costs.

Foreclosures are risky for part-time, busy investors.

Beware of the motivated seller.

5

WHERE TO BUY

MOST NOVICE REAL ESTATE INVESTORS ARE TOLD TO "INVEST only within 30 minutes of where you live." In high-priced markets this doesn't make sense. When the mortgage payment on an investment property greatly exceeds the rent one can expect as income, there's no point to investing. If you follow the 30-minute rule, you may have to wait years before the market in which you live becomes viable. Looking nationally, there's always an appropriate market in which to invest.

There are numerous markets in the U.S. where quality homes in good neighborhoods can be purchased for less then $150,000 and produce a break-even or positive cash-flow right from the start, despite using high leverage. In this age of email, fax machines and overnight mail, we can, much to the horror of the old sages, expand our horizons well beyond the 30-minute boundary and buy rental property on a nationwide basis.

The Five Essential Criteria of a Good Market

The importance of location, location, location can't be overestimated. Buying in a good market is a kind of insurance policy for your investment.

What is a good market? From years of purchasing properties all across the U.S., I've distilled the main features of a good market down to five.

PAUSE: The Five Features of a Good Market

Big City
Good Rental Market Where the Numbers Work
Not a Booming Market
Low Median Price
Sun Belt

Big City

A big city has economic diversity that ensures stability. In a small town, there might be only one source of employment, and if it goes out of business, then the rental market is ruined. In addition, a big city offers numerous property management firms. This means that property managers are more competitive, with better services and rates.

A Good Rental Market Where the Numbers Work

A good market has single family homes that rent at a certain percentage of their value; generally, where a $100,000 home will rent for $1000 a month, and a $150,000 home will rent for $1250 or so. (For more on property cash-flow analysis, see "Making the Numbers Work" in Chapter 10.)

Not a Booming Market

A booming market is not where you want to invest. By "booming," I don't just mean that prices are rising rapidly. Booming implies that there are numerous offers for each property; it also implies a kind of frantic public mind-set, in which people feel that they must buy right away, before home prices rise higher. In a booming market you'll have to compete with many other buyers, and may not get the best price for the home. It's OK to buy in a market where prices are steadily going up, but not one in which prices are escalating rapidly.

Low Median Price

High-priced markets such as San Francisco and Los Angeles are not good places to buy. First, the numbers don't work: the rental prices are too low in comparison with the monthly mortgage payments. And second, expensive homes require jumbo loans. A jumbo loan is a loan for an amount above $275,000; to secure a jumbo loan as an investor (not owner-occupier), you must use a 25% down payment. In other words, a $350,000 property would require a minimum down payment of $87,500—a rather large chunk of change for the average investor. A good market will have a median home price of $140,000 to $200,000.

Sun Belt

The recent census shows that the Sun Belt is the fastest growing region of the country. Its warm weather and lower housing costs make it very attractive to retirees. As Baby Boomers retire, we can expect the Sun Belt to grow even more.

The retirees of the future will be quite different from those of the past. They'll travel and play sports. They'll eat out often and attend cultural events. Tomorrow's retirees will insist upon a broad range of activities, and will create jobs in the areas in which they settle. All of this indicates economic stability and long-term growth. Buying in Sun Belt markets will help ensure that your investment will continue to grow over the long-term.

In addition, most Sun Belt states have a strong pro-business attitude with less taxation and are inviting the relocation of major companies. They also have landlord-tenant laws that don't heavily favor the tenant. If it becomes necessary to evict a tenant, you'll find that it can be done expeditiously—unlike in California or New York, where a knowledgeable tenant can reside at your property without paying rent for up to one year.

The Best Markets in the U.S.

Now that you know the five essential criteria of a good market, you may be wondering if any place like this actually exists. In fact, there are currently seven cities in the U.S. that have all the above features.

If you've got the time, you could do lots of research and possibly discover a few more. But you're busy. That's OK, because I've already done the research for you.

The Best U.S. Real Estate Investment Markets:

Phoenix, Arizona
Orlando, Florida
Las Vegas, Nevada
Tampa, Florida
Jacksonville, Florida
San Antonio, Texas

The Paralysis of Over-Analysis

People find all sorts of reasons for not investing in real estate. One is the fear that, unless they make a "perfect" deal, one in which all of the elements are just right, it won't work and they'll lose their shirt.

But a deal doesn't have to be the deal of the century for it to work for you. For example, an investor I know called me up recently and said, "I read an article in the newspaper yesterday that said Naples, Florida was the best market in the country. I don't want to buy in Phoenix and Orlando any more, just Naples."

First, what suddenly turned Naples into the best market in the country? It had shot up dramatically in the past year, which meant that it was no longer a great place to buy. He was shooting himself in the foot!

Second, who cares about the article? Next week there will be an article about Dallas...and the week after that,

Albuquerque.

Trying to keep tabs on the "best" market in the country is a big waste of your time. It's more important to find a good market, buy there, and stay there. When people ask me, "What's the best market in the country?" I always answer, "It's infinitely better to buy a house in the third best market in the country than not to buy a house in the best market in the country." Just do it, already! If you believe that Little Rock, Arkansas is a good market, just do it and get on with your life.

You can't enjoy the benefits of real estate if you don't own real estate! I would much rather see you buy five homes in Little Rock than talk for 20 years about buying homes in Phoenix. It always surprises me how many people fall into the trap of doing nothing. I call it the "paralysis of over-analysis." They buy books, tapes, and go to seminars…but they don't buy real estate.

Don't make yourself crazy looking for the best of all possible deals in the best of all possible markets. Just remember the five essential criteria, then spend your weekends having some fun.

> **PAUSE: Five Main Features
> of a Good Neighborhood**
>
> Safe
> Good schools
> Convenient shopping
> Majority of homes owned by residents
> Composed primarily of single family homes

Breaking the 30-Minute Rule

When people consider buying an investment home that's out of town or even out of state, they have a lot of questions: Isn't it risky? How will I check on the property? How will I handle repairs and maintenance? What if the house doesn't rent?

Allow me to address these concerns one at a time.

Risk

There's no such thing as a completely risk-free investment, of any kind, but there are ways to reduce risk when purchasing real estate. When you buy in a good market with the five essential criteria, you're already "insuring" your investment. In addition, buying a quality home located in a good neighborhood also reduces risk. A quality property needs fewer repairs than one that's in bad shape. In a good neighborhood, your tenants will be more likely to stay longer, to pay on time, and to take care of the property.

Checking Up

The last thing you want, of course, is for your house to become damaged or run-down. It may seem that making an investment closer to home would provide some reassurance that things aren't going to hell in a handbasket.

Quality properties located in good markets and in good neighborhoods will get along without your constant vigilance very well—just as they would if they were located down the street from you. And even if your investment home is nearby, it's not as if you have the right to intrude on your tenants every few weeks and make a spot check of the premises. So what are you going to do, drive by and gawk?

I can tell you right now, your house isn't going to look a lot different from month to month. Notwithstanding an Act of God, as insurance underwriters call earthquakes, tornadoes and hurricanes, etc., that's the thing about houses: they don't change much and they have a tendency to stay put.

Repairs and Maintenance

There is absolutely no law that says real estate investors need to be all-purpose handymen or women. I personally haven't picked up a hammer in years. For me, changing a light bulb is a major home improvement.

If you're like me, or even if you're a master carpenter who looks forward to the next remodeling project with unrestrained glee, do you really want to take on the burden of keeping your rental homes in tip-top shape?

No! You're busy!

So how do you take care of your investment home without spending your weekends painting, carpeting, or fixing the plumbing?

You hire a property manager.

Even if your property is located near you, this is something I highly recommend. Property managers are pros. They know a lot more about taking care of your investment home than you do.

Traditionally, there's been a lot of resistance to this idea, but I've found that this resistance is largely based on ignorance. We all hire professionals for different aspects of our lives, from attorneys and CPAs to housekeepers and pet-sitters. Hiring a property manager is no different: he or she provides us with expertise that we don't have. Why is it acceptable to hire professionals for so many other purposes, but not to hire a professional to take care of our real estate investments? Strictly speaking, if you were involved in a lawsuit, could you go to the law library and research the law? Of course. But would you do it? Of course not. Strictly speaking, could you manage your own house? Of course. But should you do it? Probably not.

Let a professional manage your property, even if it's close to where you live. This frees you up to live the life you want. Who really has the time or the desire to be a "hands-on" landlord? Not me! I own dozens of homes spread all across the country. If I didn't use property managers, I'd never have the time to run a business, write a book, or do anything else.

In fact, I'd probably be repairing a toilet at this very moment.

Vacancies

One of your biggest fears may be that your house is not going to rent. When you buy a quality home in a good market, you minimize this risk.

The vacancy problem I encounter most often is not that the house is unrentable, it's that the owners are asking for too much rent. They haven't listened to the local experts, such as their realtor and property manager, and have insisted on listing the rental above what the market will bear—usually because they feel that their house is, well, special.

It's much better to live with a little bit of negative cash flow than to price your rental so high that it stands vacant. You don't have to "squeeze" the house for every nickel and dime in order to be getting something of great value back from your investment. Your tax benefits will go a long way towards off-setting any negative cash flow you may have in the first year or two. It's inevitable that rental prices will increase with the cost of living, and change that negative into a positive.

Still, you'll want to take into account the vacancy rate for the market into which you've bought. For some of the markets I've mentioned above, the average vacancy rate for quality single family homes is 3%, which means that, statistically, your house will be vacant for three months out of one hundred. If the rent is $1000 per month, then you can deduct $30 from your cash flow figures. If you want to play it really safe, deduct $50.

Just remember that there's usually no such thing as an unrented house, there's only asking for too much rent.

Buy Where it Makes Sense to Buy

All I'm saying here is that the best way for you to ensure that your investment will be a good one is to buy where it makes sense to buy: in a good market, and in a good neighborhood.

When I began investing, I bought lower-priced homes that weren't always so well located. Yes, they were "bargains." And you know what? If I'd started out buying quality homes in good neighborhoods, I would've made a lot more money by now, and had fewer headaches. I can't stress it strongly enough: buy quality homes in good neighborhoods. It's one of the primary keys to making your investments work for you, and not the other way around.

Since a professional property manager is going to be looking after your property, why not buy where it makes sense to buy? Just because you happen to go to sleep at night in Los Angeles, does that mean that all of your investments have to be in Los Angeles?

REPLAY

You can't enjoy the benefits of real estate if you don't own real estate!

Break the 30-minute rule, and buy where it makes sense to buy.

Keep in mind the 5 essential criteria: Big City, Good Rental Market where the Numbers Work, Not a Booming Market, Low Median Price, Sun Belt.

It's much better to invest in a good market than not to invest in the "best" market.

Don't let the "paralysis of over-analysis" stop you from investing.

A deal doesn't have to be the deal of the century for it to work for you.

Use professional property management to look after your properties.

There's usually no such thing as an unrented house, there's only asking for too much rent.

Buy quality homes in good neighborhoods.

6

GETTING STARTED

JUST AS EVERY JOURNEY BEGINS WITH A SINGLE STEP, THE ROAD to your financial well-being begins with a single and attainable goal: buying your first investment home.

In a very real sense, buying your first investment home is the biggest hurdle. After all, you're traveling in uncharted territory, the new world of real estate investing. No doubt you'll have many questions, and even, perhaps, a few fears. But as you go through the process of buying your first investment home, your questions will be answered and your fears put to rest. I've found that something else happens when you take this step: an increased confidence and sense of empowerment that comes from taking control of your financial future.

In this chapter I'm going to encourage you to take stock of your finances and show you what you should have in place before you purchase your first investment home. Whether you've already got money set aside or you need to raise money before you start, you'll find some handy tips for getting on the right track and staying there.

Becoming Financially Fit

Financial fitness is the basis of sound financial planning. By financially fit, I don't mean wealthy. What I mean instead is that you have a solid understanding of your overall financial picture and a feasible budget that includes funds for investing. Becoming financially fit means knowing where you need to go, and knowing how you'll get there.

Before you begin investing, it's a good idea to take a careful look at "the big picture": what you own, what you owe, and how much cash and credit are available to you. To do this, you'll need to calculate your net worth and analyze your expenditures. Your annual income, the amount of debt you carry, your spending habits and your attitude about money will all play a part in the way you invest and how you structure your financial plan.

What is Net Worth?

Your net worth is the wealth you've accumulated to date: the amount that's left over after subtracting your liabilities from your assets. Assets include cash and savings, your home and personal property, stocks and bonds, real estate, privately owned businesses and retirement accounts. Liabilities include mortgage(s), car loans or lease, student or other loans, and credit card debt.

Your net worth is your financial barometer. It reveals the reserves you have to tap into—or the opposite, how your liabilities may be undermining your assets.

NET WORTH WORKSHEET

ASSETS

CASH AND SAVINGS $ _____

INVESTMENTS
STOCKS & MUTUAL FUNDS
BONDS & BOND MUTUAL FUNDS
STOCK OPTIONS
VALUE OF PRIVATELY OWNED BUSINESS
INVESTMENT REAL ESTATE
CASH VALUE OF LIFE INSURANCE POLICIES
OTHER INVESTMENTS
TOTAL INVESTMENTS $ _____

RETIREMENT ACCOUNTS
IRAs
401(k), 401(b)
SELF-EMPLOYED PLANS (Keogh, etc.)
ANNUITIES
EST. VALUE OF COMPANY PENSION
TOTAL RETIREMENT ACCOUNTS $ _____

HOME & PERSONAL PROPERTY
HOME
VACATION HOME
CARS, RECREATIONAL VEHICLES
ART, COLLECTIBLES, JEWELRY, FURNISHINGS
OTHER PERSONAL ASSETS
TOTAL HOME & PERSONAL PROPERTY $ _____

TOTAL ASSETS $ _____

LIABILITIES
MORTGAGE DEBT
CAR LOANS/LEASE
STUDENT LOANS
CREDIT CARD BALANCES
OTHER LOANS
OTHER DEBT
TOTAL LIABILITIES $ _____

NET WORTH (subtract liabilities from assets) $ _____

Once you've calculated your net worth, you will see at a glance how your assets and liabilities stack up. While there's no hard-and-fast rule about how much you should have, or the percentage of liabilities to assets, you may discover some surprises. Perhaps your credit card debt has just about wiped out the positive figures in the assets section. Perhaps your home equity, stocks or retirement accounts have grown more than you anticipated. Your net worth statement shows you how your assets and your debts are distributed. When it comes time to raise cash or apply for a loan, this information will be very helpful to you.

PAUSE: It's important to update your net worth statement on a regular basis, typically once a year. It's a good way to keep in touch with your financial goals, and to make sure you're on the right path. Watching your net worth increase will help you stay focused, and keep your enthusiasm high. Long-term investing requires discipline, and sometimes it can feel as if the rewards don't come soon enough. Your net worth statement transforms the abstract into black and white: you'll see the results of your hard work on the bottom line.

Insurance Coverage

An important part of financial fitness is making sure that you and your assets are protected. Comprehensive insurance coverage is your primary defense against unforeseen—and potentially disastrous—events. It's true that insurance premiums take a bite out of your budget and may seem, at times, like an unnecessary expense. Without proper insurance, however, you're gambling with your future, and with what you've already worked so hard to achieve.

There are four major areas of your life that need to be insured against loss: yourself, your dependents, your potential earnings, and your property.

Health Insurance

If you're fortunate, your employer has a group plan to which you can subscribe, and your premiums may be included in your salary and benefits. Group plans generally offer the best coverage at the lowest price.

If you're self-employed, or if you can't get health insurance through your employer, you may want to contact a health insurance broker. You can find one in the yellow pages. Brokers will have access to a range of companies, and can help you find a plan that fits your circumstances and budget.

Life Insurance

Life insurance provides some peace of mind for those with dependents. Steer clear of "whole" or "universal" life insurance: the investment account associated with this kind of policy is usually low on returns and high on commissions. Go for term life insurance instead, basing your coverage amount on your income times the number of years you plan to keep working until retirement.

Disability Insurance

Your future income-earning ability is one of your biggest assets. If, because of illness or accident, you're unable to work, disability insurance will replace some or all of your lost income. Large companies often offer disability insurance to employees. If you're self-employed, you can find disability insurance through an insurance carrier or through a state-funded program. Check with insurance companies and your state disability insurance office to compare premiums and coverage.

Property Insurance

Homes, cars, and other property should be insured for their replacement cost. In addition, liability coverage protects you against lawsuits. Homeowners and auto insurance generally comes with a certain amount of liability coverage; check your records to make sure it's adequate. You may also want to look into "umbrella" or excess liability insurance: a good rule of thumb is to insure yourself for at least twice the amount of your net worth.

Retirement Accounts

If you're eligible for an IRA plan, 401(k), 403(b), SEP, Keogh or any other tax-deferred retirement plan, by all means, take advantage of it. These plans offer tax shelters, which means immediate benefits, and the power of compounding, which means long-term benefits. As with any account that grows through compounding—or interest earned on interest earned—the sooner you start, the more you stand to gain.

Using the investment options available to you is the surest way to become financially fit. Just because you've decided to invest in real estate doesn't mean that you should ignore other viable investments. Basically, a retirement plan is a high-yield, favorably taxed, long-term savings account. Ideally, your financial strategy will include both a retirement account and real estate investments; the two are not mutually exclusive, but complementary.

How Much Money You'll Need to Get Started

Although many books and infomercials insist that you can purchase real estate with "no money down," the truth is that most real estate investments require an initial outlay of cash.

Exactly how much cash depends, of course, on the price of the property, the amount of leverage you use, and the closing costs. To keep it simple, though, I suggest that you set of goal of $15,000.

Sometimes It Feels Like a Lot...

Why $15,000? Because it's enough to cover a 10% down payment and closing costs on $135,000 property, the average price of a quality single family home in the markets I've recommended.

If you happen to have $15,000 lying around already—in a savings account, money market fund, or under the mattress—you can save yourself a little time and move right along to the next chapter.

But perhaps you don't have $15,000 lying around. Perhaps you're not sure just how you're going to come up with $15,000, unless you plant a money tree in your backyard. If you're finding it difficult to sock away $50 into your savings account each month, a number with five figures can seem daunting.

...Sometimes It Don't

I know for a fact that raising $15,000 is possible for anyone. You may not be able to come up with that much money overnight, but if you keep your $15,000 goal firmly in mind, you will make it happen. Saving is just one way to raise money; there are a number of others, which I'll explain. And yes, you can purchase real estate with less cash; I'll tell you more about that, too. If you're busy, however, the straightforward approach—putting 10% down—is often the best. It may mean some belt-tightening, but that's sometimes easier, and better for your financial fitness, than financing the entire amount.

It may help to remember this: $15,000 equals real property worth $135,000. In 20 years, the property will be worth over $250,000, by the most conservative measure (assuming the house doesn't appreciate more than the cost of living). At one and a half times the current inflation rate (which is, historically, the amount that real estate appreciates each year), it will be worth over $340,000.

In other words: the $15,000 you sow today will reap over $300,000 in the future. To accumulate that much money without investing in real estate, you would have to save $15,000 every year for 20 years.

If you have a hard time imagining what it will feel like to have $300,000 20 years from now, think about this: what if, 20 years ago, you'd invested $15,000 and had that $300,000 now?

If you're like most people, you'll wish you had invested $15,000 20 years ago. I can assure you that, 20 years from now, you're going to feel exactly the same way.

Does $15,000 still sound like a lot of money?

Reaching Your First Goal: $15,000

There are three primary ways to raise money: earn it, save it, or borrow it.

Of course, you can use any combination of the three. As you look over your net worth statement and budget, you'll discover the best way for you. I've listed the various ways to raise money in ascending order, from the most conservative (earning) to the most aggressive (borrowing). You'll need to be honest with yourself, and look over your history. If you're currently trying to get out from under a load of credit card debt, the last thing you want to do is incur more. At the other end of the spectrum, if you're someone who never pays a cent in interest, you may find that you can benefit from using the credit that's available to you.

Eight Ways to Raise Money

Earn it

Save it

Sell unused assets

Borrow it

- **Equity loan**
- **Against 401(k)**
- **From friends or relatives**
- **From a bank**
- **From credit cards (beware!!!)**

Earning It

If your job and family have you constantly on the go, taking on part-time employment to earn more money is probably out of the question. But there may be things you can do that you haven't thought of, such as home sales, or a side-line hobby or craft. Or perhaps you can use your special expertise to work as a part-time consultant in your field.

If you have few assets, and a low income that's already stretched to the limit, a part-time business may be your answer. Benefits include flexibility—you can set your own hours—and tax deductions against your income, which may lead to tax savings. (You'll need to peruse Schedule C, Profit or Loss from Business, of the IRS' 1040 form to see how this may apply to your particular situation, or ask your tax preparer.)

Selling Unused Assets

A corollary to earning more income is raising money by selling items you don't want or need anymore. No, I don't mean a yard sale…but what about that boat or RV that's been gathering dust in the driveway? The time-share you never have time to use? The empty plot of land in Northern Idaho that Uncle Willie left to you? The piano no one plays?

Take a good look at the things you own. If they're not appreciating assets, and they don't have sentimental value (such as family heirlooms), you might want to consider selling them. After all, we're talking about your future. Why let your money sit around in unused assets, when it can be working for you?

Saving It

You may wonder why, no matter how much money you make, you're finding it hard to save. You're not alone. On average, people are saving only 5% of their after-tax income.

Learning to budget and allocate funds for your future is essential to becoming financially fit. In fact, the money you set aside for investments is the most important part of your budget. Unfortunately, too many people see it as the least important, something that they do only if there's enough left over—and all too often, there's nothing left over.

To make a profound difference in your future, you must reorganize your priorities, and place investment funds right up there with food, shelter and insurance. In order to do this, you'll need to look at how you've spent money in the past. Collect all your receipts from the past three months (if you're self-employed, or have a fluctuating income, you may want to go back six months), and fill out the form on the following page, or make up a list of your own.

EXPENDITURES WORKSHEET

Mortgage or Rent
Property Tax
Homeowners/Renters Insurance
Utilities
Furnishings, Maintenance
Telephone
Other Household Expenses

Groceries
Dining Out

Car Loan/Lease
Fuel, Maintenance & Repairs
Auto Insurance
Other Transportation (taxi, bus, etc.)

Federal, State, Local Taxes
Social Security or Pension Contributions
Tax on Investment Income

Retirement Plan Contributions
Passbook/Money Market Savings

Health Insurance
Medical Services, Drugs not covered by insurance
Health Club Dues

Child Care

Movies, Theater, Cable TV
Books, Magazines, Videos

Apparel, Shoes
Personal Care (haircuts, massage)
Laundry, Dry Cleaning

Vacations, Travel

Miscellaneous Expenses

TOTAL MONTHLY EXPENSES $ _____

Evaluating your spending habits is probably the most painful part of the process, but it's also one of the most enlightening. Most people are shocked when they see just how much they spend each month on things that aren't exactly necessary. If you and your spouse both work, it's probably even more of a shock. The busier you are, the more money you're likely to spend, and the less time you have to keep track of exactly how you're spending it.

There's only one way to save without earning more money, and that's to spend less. Looking over your expenditures, you're sure to find areas where you can economize. In fact, your spending habits are the first place to look for cash.

It may be time to bite the bullet, and trade off some of the luxuries you enjoy now—frequent dining out, or expensive vacations—in order to begin building your future. But don't forget to look at the little luxuries you take for granted. If you can save just $10 a day—the price of a deli lunch and a café latte—you'll save $3650 a year. If you and your spouse save $10 a day each, that's $7300—or one investment home every two years or so!

Just Say "No" to Consumer Spending

We grew up in an age of instant credit and immediate gratification. It's pretty hard to resist the appeal of buying now and paying later, and it can be a difficult habit to break. But it's one of the reasons why people are finding it hard to save and to plan for the future.

Over-use of credit for things like cars, electronics, vacations, and other life-style goodies is a big trap that's all too easy to fall into. Add up your credit card balances and car loans to see what you're paying in interest alone each year.

The money you throw away on interest isn't the only price you pay for buying now and paying later. If the new car, the wide-screen TV, and the hot tub mean that you don't have anything left over to save or invest each month, you're robbing yourself of a prosperous future.

For example, the average cost of a new car is $20,000. Even with a low interest rate, the payments will be approximately $500 a month: that's $6000 each year for five years, or $30,000. In 20 years, what will you have to show for this expense? A 20-year-old car. If, instead, you'd invested that $30,000 in real estate, you'd own property worth over $600,000.

Then, you can buy any car you want…in a few different colors.

The real, bottom-line secret to financial planning is learning to delay gratification, to live with a little less now so that you'll have more—much more—in the future. It's not complicated, and it doesn't require any special know-how, just some discipline and determination.

Creating Your New, Financially Fit Budget

Once you're recovered from the shock of your monthly expenditures, it's time to make a plan to get your spending under control. On the next page is a budget worksheet for you to fill in, or copy. Notice that "investment funds" is listed right up top, along with your mortgage, insurance premiums, and retirement accounts.

BUDGET WORKSHEET

Investment Funds _____
Retirement Plan Contributions _____
Passbook/Money Market Savings _____

Life Insurance _____
Disability Insurance _____

Mortgage or Rent _____
Property Tax _____
Homeowners/Renters Insurance _____
Utilities _____
Furnishings, Maintenance _____
Telephone _____
Other Household Expenses _____

Groceries _____
Dining Out _____

Car Loan/Lease _____
Fuel, Maintenance & Repairs _____
Auto Insurance _____
Other Transportation (taxi, bus, etc.) _____

Federal, State, Local Taxes _____
Social Security or Pension Contributions _____
Tax on Investment Income _____

Health Insurance _____
Medical Services, Drugs not covered by insurance _____
Health Club Dues _____

Child Care _____

Movies, Theater, Cable TV _____
Books, Magazines, Videos _____

Apparel, Shoes _____
Personal Care (haircuts, massage) _____
Laundry, Dry Cleaning _____

Vacations, Travel _____

TOTAL MONTHLY BUDGET $_____

Create a budget that re-prioritizes your expenses, and places money for investment before other expenses such as clothing, dining out, entertainment, and other areas in your budget that you may be able to cut back on.

Set Up a Separate Account

Opening a separate account for your investment funds is an excellent way to keep your budget on track and your goal firmly in sight. Whether you're saving in order to buy your first investment home or to finance further investments, decide on a set amount that you can deposit each month, and stick to it.

If you're on an accelerated savings plan, or already have some cash set aside, a regular savings account will do. However, a money market fund (available from mutual fund companies), combines the convenience of a savings or checking account with a higher yield, or return, on your money.

When you contribute to a money market fund, you're actually buying shares in a large portfolio of money market securities such as Treasury bills, commercial paper, and other cash equivalents. As with a savings account, your money is safe (the principal is not at risk), and liquid (you can make deposits and withdrawals just as you can with a savings or checking account), but a money market fund will grow at a faster rate than a savings account.

Another Way to Save

If you have a hard time sticking to a budget, there may be a way to save that will work for you: enlist the government's help.

If you have a tendency to spend all your income every month, reduce the number of tax exemptions on your W-2 form. More tax dollars will be taken out of each paycheck, which you'll get back, months later, in the form of a tax refund.

This isn't the best way to save, because the feds, and not you, earn interest on the money that's deducted from your earnings. Of course, when you get your refund, it has to go straight into your money market fund or savings account. And in the meantime, put away those credit cards!

If, on the other hand, you receive a large refund each year, you may want to increase the number of exemptions. With more exemptions, fewer tax dollars will be taken out of your paycheck, and you can put the extra into your money market fund. This way, you can watch your investment account grow each month, and earn dividends while you're saving.

Borrowing It

If you don't have cash on hand, and you'd like to start investing right away, borrowing may be the answer. The sooner you begin investing, the sooner you'll see benefits, so I always recommend taking action as quickly as possible (with a few caveats).

If you've got friends or relatives with deep pockets, they may be willing to finance a down payment. If you have equity in your home, 401(k), or other retirement account, you may be able to borrow against your own assets. If you have good credit and a steady income, you may be able to borrow from a bank.

There are pros and cons to each of these methods. But before you contemplate taking on more debt, take a look at the debt you already have. What are your monthly payments? Will you be able to take on an additional monthly payment, and still adhere to your new, financially fit budget? If you have credit card debt, are you just paying the minimum every month, or are you able to pay them off in full?

If you're already carrying a lot of debt—especially credit card debt—you should consider consolidating or paying off those debts before taking on more.

Borrowing from Friends or Relatives

Hitting up a rich friend or relative may be a fast and easy way to raise the cash you need to get started. If your parents are financially secure, they may be more than willing to offer you a loan, especially after you've shown them that it will be used to finance a serious, sound, long-term investment.

Before you begin calling up everyone you know, consider how borrowing money from friends or relatives might affect your relationship. Think about what may happen if, for some reason, you're unable to pay it back. And what if your benefactor suddenly goes broke and needs the money returned right away?

As long as everything goes exactly as planned, borrowing from a friend or relative can give you a head start. Chances are they'll offer favorable rates, or even a tax-free gift of up to $10,000. But the unforeseen does sometimes happen, and if you want to maintain good relationships, you'll make sure that all involved parties have a complete understanding of the terms of the loan.

Put everything in writing: the loan amount, interest rate, and payment schedule. Discuss all possibilities that may arise, and how you'll deal with them. And put that in writing, too.

Borrowing from Home Equity

Equity is the difference between your home's current market value and the amount you owe. Your net worth statement should show you how much equity you have in your home.

Assuming that you can afford the monthly payments of a second mortgage, and your current debt load is not too great, an equity loan is perhaps the easiest and most cost-effective way to borrow money from yourself.

Many lenders offer equity loans. Because the loan is secured against your property, interest rates for equity loans are generally lower than rates for unsecured loans. In addition, the interest you pay on an equity loan is usually tax-deductible.

Borrowing from Retirement Plans

Some retirement plans allow you to borrow money against your retirement account to buy a home; whether or not you can is dependent on the plan managers who set it up.

The advantage of borrowing against your retirement account to raise a down-payment is that you'll be paying back your own account, with interest, rather than paying interest to a mortgage company. The disadvantage is that, if you don't pay the loan back in a specified amount of time, the loan is considered a distribution. If you're under 59 1/2 years of age, you'll have to pay a penalty plus income taxes on the amount you borrowed.

Borrowing from a Bank

In these times of mergers and consolidations, when local banks are swallowed up by national corporations, it's harder than ever to qualify for a bank loan. Even if the local branch manager is your tennis buddy, chances are your loan application will be sent to a loan service center in another state. It will be processed by a computer that cares about only three things: your social security number, your annual income and your credit rating.

If you have a high annual income and good credit rating, the computer might spit out a favorable answer. Otherwise, you're just plain out of luck. Computers don't care about extenuating factors, such as your trustworthiness, your willingness to give up vacations for the next five years, or the fact that your grandmother is rich and you'll inherit her fortune (of course, if that's true, you may not need the bank after all). Typically, the bank manager can't override the decision of the ultimate number-cruncher.

It may seem that the old adage is true now more than ever: banks only lend money to those who don't need it.

Is there a way to get around this? Yes and no. If it means playing a kind of round-robin game by opening as many credit lines in as many banks as possible, then no. File that idea under hare-brained scheme (and that may be an injustice to rabbit intelligence). Unless you're a financial wizard, playing games with banks and multiple lines of credit is a sure way to mess up your credit rating.

In case you haven't noticed it, banks are not very playful. It's better to approach them as you would an unfriendly giant that you hope to recruit as a player for your basketball team. You've got to woo him a little, and offer him his favorite food—in this case, your money.

Having a relationship with your bank is the best way to establish yourself as a worthy loan applicant. By relationship, I don't mean dinners and flowers, but keeping all your accounts in the same place, and getting to know the bank manager and loan officers. If you feel like small potatoes at your current bank, look for a smaller, more local operation that may be more appreciative of your business. Every time you need a loan, be it a home equity loan, car loan or business loan, look to your bank for financing. After a few secured loans that you pay back on time, they'll get to know you as a safe credit risk. In the world of banking relationships, that's a good as being engaged.

Borrowing from Credit Cards (Beware!!!)

Borrowing money from credit cards is an option, but not one that I recommend. Credit card money is probably the most expensive money you can borrow. Credit cards charge high interest, and the interest you pay is not tax deductible.

Before you take cash advances from your credit cards, consider whether another way to borrow is available to you. Any one of the other possibilities outlined above is better for your financial fitness.

If borrowing from credit cards is the only way for you to

raise a down payment for your first investment home, be certain that you meet the following criteria:

1) You have excellent credit, and you plan to keep it that way.

2) You have very little outstanding debt.

3) You can afford the extra payments.

4) You're responsible. *Very* responsible.

In other words, you have enough income, and enough discipline, to pay off the amount drawn from your credit cards within a few months. If you allow the credit card balances to remain much longer than that, you're going to pay a very steep price.

Above all, be aware of the cost involved before you borrow.

What "No Money Down" Really Means

What "no money down" really means is that the property is 100% leveraged. In other words, the purchaser has borrowed the entire amount, including the down payment, to buy the property.

In the "no money down" method that gained popularity a few years back, financing is offered by the seller. In my experience, seller financing is not nearly as widespread as some would have you believe. Just because it's possible doesn't make it probable. The overwhelming majority of people who sell their homes need to cash out.

Another thing rarely mentioned is the type of property offered by sellers who are willing to finance. Quality single family homes in good markets rarely, if ever, have motivated sellers. Unfortunately, the "gurus" have made buying with no money down more important than buying quality real estate. In the final analysis, how you finance the property isn't as important as buying real estate that will be a sound, long-term investment: in other words, quality homes in good neighborhoods. Even if it's 100% financed, a bad property is still a bad property!

Five No Money Down Techniques

The types of borrowing I've mentioned above are actually no money down techniques. When you borrow the down payment from:

- a friend or family member,
- your own home equity,
- a retirement account,
- a bank
- or credit cards,

that's also 100% leverage, or no money down.

If 100% leverage works for you, by all means, do it. Remember, however, it will mean that you'll have higher monthly payments, and may have to live with negative cash flow for a while. However, this may lower your tax liability, which could mitigate the negative cash flow somewhat. If your budget can handle it, and it's the only way for you to begin investing, then you may want to consider it.

REPLAY

Buying one investment home should be your first goal.

Becoming financially fit means understanding your overall financial picture, and setting goals.

Comprehensive insurance coverage is your primary defense against unforeseen events.

Contribute to at least one retirement plan.

The $15,000 you sow today will reap over $300,000 in 20 years.

Learning to budget and allocate funds for investing is essential to your financial fitness.

Just say "no" to consumer spending.

Set up a separate account for investment funds.

Know the cost of borrowing before you borrow.

No Money Down simply means 100% financing.

7

FINANCING

EVEN IF YOU'RE ABLE TO PAY CASH FOR AN INVESTMENT property, it isn't in your best interest to do so. Financing the property often means using leverage, long-term fixed-rate loans, and gaining tax benefits: the troika that makes your money and net worth grow.

In this chapter, I'll explain the loan types you should choose from, what lenders look for in a borrower, the importance of good credit, and the documents you'll need to complete your loan application.

Selecting a Mortgage

Financing is all too often a stressful and confusing part of purchasing your investment home. There are so many mortgage lenders, offering an ever-increasing number of loan options, that it can be difficult to know where to begin. Throw in financing jargon—points, prepaids, APR, PMI, caps, etc.—

and you might wish you never started.

Happily, you don't need to be a financial wizard or a mortgage maven in order to secure favorable financing for your investment property. Financing doesn't have to be complicated. Even though many loan types are available, there are only three types of loans that I recommend. Any one of these common loan types will provide you with long-term, safe, secure financing with no unpleasant surprises.

Fixed-Rate Mortgages

When you get a fixed-rate mortgage, you know exactly what your monthly payments will be. No matter what the term of the loan, your payments will not change.

A 30-year loan offers the most flexibility. Since the payments are lower than a 15-year loan, it frees up more of your income for other purposes, such as funding retirement accounts or other investments. Or you can make extra payments on the principal and pay off the loan sooner. In fact, the 30-year loan contains the 15-year loan, or the 18-year loan, or the 10-year loan: you can pay it off in the number of years that fits your financial plan.

Fixed-rate loans generally carry a slightly higher interest rate than adjustable or short-term loans, because the lender is making a commitment to lend money at a fixed rate over a long term. Remember, however, that inflation will effectively reduce the amount of your mortgage payment year after year. A fixed-rate loan with a payment that does not change over the life of your investment will provide you with a monthly payment that will erode over time.

It probably goes without saying that you'll want the lowest interest rate possible, although there are a few other things to consider when selecting a loan (see "Shopping for a Loan," later in this chapter). But not everyone will qualify for the lowest interest rate available; the rate you're offered will depend upon your credit worthiness and other factors. If the interest rate for fixed-rate loans is high (above 8.5%), or if the only fixed-rate loan you can qualify for is two or three points above the best rate, then you may want to consider two other financing options: an adjustable rate mortgage or a hybrid mortgage.

Adjustable-Rate Mortgages

Adjustable-rate mortgages (ARMs) have a variable interest rate that rises or falls according to the index to which they are tied. Most ARMs adjust annually, but some adjust monthly, or every six months.

The first-year rate (or "teaser" rate) of an ARM is usually a point or two below the interest rate for fixed-rate loans. The interest rate on many, but not all, ARMs is capped, meaning that it can rise only a certain number of percentage points, usually five, over the life of the loan. For instance, if your starting interest rate is 6%, and you have a five-point cap, then the highest interest rate possible on your ARM is 11%.

The rise of the interest rate on an ARM is limited to either one or two percentage points each year, so the interest rate can't rise from 6% to 11% overnight, but would take several years to rise to its highest rate. An ARM can also go down, if the index to which it is tied goes down.

ARMS can be beneficial when rates on fixed-rate loans are high (above 8.5%), or if you can't qualify for a low interest fixed-rate loan. Because you usually know when and how much your ARM is going to rise, you can begin with an ARM, then refinance a few years later, when the interest rate on a fixed-rate loan is lower than your ARM. By then, you'll have equity in the property, and it may be easier for you to qualify for a lower interest fixed-rate loan.

Hybrid Loans

As the name implies, hybrid loans are a combination of fixed-rate and adjustable loans. Hybrid loans, also called intermediate ARMs, start out like a fixed-rate loan, with a fixed interest rate for a term of three, five, or seven years (they're generally referred to, respectively, as a 3/1, 5/1 and 7/1; a pure ARM is often referred to as a 1/1). After the initial term, the loan converts to an ARM, adjusting every six to 12 months.

The starting interest rate of a hybrid loan, like an ARM, is lower than a fixed-rate loan, but because it's locked in for a longer time than the six-month or one-year teaser rate of an ARM, it's higher than an adjustable.

During times when fixed-rate loans have low interest rates, the difference between ARMS, hybrids and fixed-rate loans can be as little as one or one-half percent. During these periods, fixed-rate loans offer the best long-term value. When interest rates rise, and the difference between fixed-rate and adjustable rate loans is greater, then ARMS and hybrids can offer considerable savings—at least for the first few years.

Take on an adjustable or hybrid loan only if you can't qualify for a 30-year, fixed-rate loan or when interest rates for fixed-rates loans are high. If you do this, however, refinance to a 30-year, fixed-rate loan when interest rates decline and it's possible to lock-in a low rate. Refinancing does have some costs involved, but they are usually recouped over time when you refinance to a lower rate. Also, in many cases the refinancing costs can be included in the new loan balance so that you don't have to pay cash for them, but instead borrow the refinancing costs at a low rate over 30 years.

PAUSE: Why I Recommend 30-year, Fixed-Rate Loans

As an investor, your safest course is to go with a fixed-rate loan. This keeps your payments stable over the life of your investment, which helps you to estimate cash flow, expenses, profits, taxes, and so on. But my main reason for recommending it is that the cost of a 30-year fixed-rate erodes as the cost of living rises. Don't be scared of the 30-year term. You can pay the loan off at any time—after 5, 11 or 16 years—usually without paying a penalty. 30-year, fixed rate financing is the ultimate no-brainer. Once you have it in place, you don't have to think about it again.

Shopping for a Loan: Comparing Costs

The cost of a mortgage involves more than just interest rates. The loan package, or "product," as it's known in the industry, consists of an interest rate, points, and loan-related fees. Points are always paid at settlement, or "closing," as it's generally called. So are many of the fees, hence the term "closing costs." (See "Making an Offer" in Chapter 10 for a complete explanation of escrow and closing.)

The annual percentage rate, or APR, is the combination of the loan's interest rate, points and fees, and indicates the "true" cost of the loan. If all lenders used the same method to calculate APRs, selecting the lowest-priced loan would be easy. Unfortunately, they don't. The only way to know the actual cost of a loan is to know the price of the fees associated with that loan.

Within three days of your loan application, the lender is required to provide you with a Good Faith Estimate, which is an estimate of the points and fees charged by the lender. You can compare the cost of loans—assuming that the interest rates and terms are the same—by applying to two or more lenders and comparing the fees outlined in the lenders' Good Faith Estimates. Along with the Good Faith Estimate, you should receive a Truth in Lending Disclosure document, which describes the loan in detail including the interest rate, the APR, and any adjustable rate features that may apply.

Points and Fees

A point is an up-front fee paid to the lender at closing. One point equals one percent of the loan amount. For example, one point of a $100,000 mortgage would be $1000, two points would be $2000, and so on.

There are two kinds of points. Origination points are for processing the loan; typically, one point, or one percent of the loan amount, is charged for this service.

Discount points are paid by the borrower to reduce the interest rate of the loan. It's common to be offered a choice of loans with various combinations of interest rates and points; the more points, the lower the rate, and vice versa. As the borrower, you can decide whether you're better off paying a higher interest rate or "buying down" the rate by paying points at closing.

Loan fees fall into one of two groups. The first group includes amounts paid to state and local governments, including city, county and state recordation fees, and prepaid property taxes. The second group includes the costs of getting a mortgage, with fees for title insurance, appraisals, credit checks, loan origination and documentation fees, commitment and processing fees, hazard and mortgage insurance, title insurance and interest prepayments.

The payments to state and local governments should be the same at every lender. The fees in the second group, however, can vary from lender to lender, and are a substantial part of your loan cost.

Because closing practices vary from region to region, it's difficult to provide accurate estimates for these costs. Typically, they range from 2.5% to 5% of the loan amount. You can shop around for competitive pricing, and in some instances, you can negotiate lower fees. Especially negotiable items include document preparation fees and lender's attorney fees.

Don't forget that points and interest rates are also negotiable. The mortgage industry is very competitive, and a lender won't deny a loan to an approved borrower just because you asked for a 25% discount on the points (they might say no to your request, but they won't refuse the loan). You won't know if it's possible to get a better deal unless you ask!

Private Mortgage Insurance: To Pay or Not to Pay?

When you make a down-payment of less than 20 percent, lenders require that you carry private mortgage insurance, or PMI. Common (mortgage industry) wisdom holds that borrowers who have less than a 20% stake in their property are more likely to default. Private mortgage insurance protects lenders (not borrowers) from financial loss when a homeowner goes into foreclosure.

Typically, a portion of the PMI premium is paid at closing, and a monthly payment representing 1/12 of the annual premium is paid along with the principal and interest of the loan. For an investment property, PMI averages 1.04 percent of the loan amount. For example, on a $100,000 loan, the annual PMI premium would be $1040, with monthly payments of $86.66.

The cost of PMI for investment properties is higher than for owner-occupied properties and, for this reason, some investors prefer to use a 20% down-payment instead of 10%, and avoid PMI altogether. On the flip side, I've often financed investment properties with 10% down, paid PMI, and still had a positive monthly cash-flow.

Personally, I prefer to use as much leverage as possible; that additional 10% down-payment could be used to purchase another investment property. Remember that PMI can be cancelled as soon as you have more than 25% equity in the property (this figure applies to investors; homeowners only need 20% equity), which could be as soon as two to three years in a good market. Even if it takes longer, say five years, the PMI on a $100,000 loan adds up to just $5200 spread over five years.

Generally, when you compare the price of PMI to $11,000 cash out of your pocket, the PMI wins. However, if you're older, have a lot of cash, and need cash flow right away, use a 20% or 30% down payment and skip the PMI.

A Third Financing Scenario

There's another option that's currently popular. In this scenario, you put only 10% down, and you don't pay PMI. Sounds good? Thank a creative mortgage banker.

It's called the 80/10/10 mortgage. (Mortgage bankers are creative with numbers, apparently, but not with names.) It's actually two mortgages: the first, which is an 80% loan-to-value mortgage, and the second, which is a loan for an additional 10% of the property's value. The last "10" refers to your down-payment.

The first loan is a 30-year, fixed-rate mortgage. The second, 10% loan is financed for a shorter term, usually 15 years, at a higher rate.

The rates and terms of an 80/10/10 can vary, so it's advisable to carefully compare the cost of the 80/10/10 against the cost of traditional financing with PMI. One advantage of the 80/10/10, however, is that the interest on the second mortgage is tax-deductible, whereas PMI is not.

Where Do Mortgages Come From?

So, where do you go to get a loan? These days, finding a lender isn't hard; in fact, there's a bewildering number out there. If you already own a home, you're probably inundated with daily offers for equity, home improvement, and debt consolidation loans.

Lenders can be grouped into two categories: commercial banks, credit unions, and savings and loan associations; and mortgage banks.

Commercial banks, credit unions and savings and loan associations are the first places most people think of when contemplating mortgages, but they don't always offer the most favorable rates. If you're a member of a credit union or have sizeable accounts at a bank or savings and loan, however, it may be worthwhile to inquire about their loan products and pricing.

Mortgage banks are companies that originate, close and service mortgage loans. Unlike the financial institutions mentioned above, they don't offer traditional bank services. Since they focus solely on making mortgage loans, they generally offer attractive programs and rates.

A Recommended Option: Mortgage Brokers

Mortgage brokers are intermediaries between borrowers and lenders. Typically, they have access to a wide variety of lenders, including commercial banks and mortgage banks, and can offer you a choice of loans. Brokers can help you complete your loan application, and can explain any differences between the loans that are offered to you. If you're turned down by a lender, they can quickly place your application with another lender, and speed up the approval process.

Although most brokers charge a fee for their service (some are paid a commission by the lender), they can save you money by shopping your loan application to various lenders. They can also save you a great deal of time. They're in the middle of the mortgage market every day, and will (or should) know a competitively-priced loan when they see it. They know how to talk to lenders, and will be able to explain the sometimes mystifying jargon of all those loan documents you've got to sign.

Another advantage of working with a broker is that you won't have to create a new loan application package every time you apply to a lender. They'll have your loan application and supporting documents on file, ready to go the next time you apply for a loan with, perhaps, just a little updating.

For all these reasons I recommend finding a trustworthy, dedicated broker with whom you can establish a long-term working relationship. Tell them that you're planning to create a portfolio of investment homes; if you have a timetable in mind (i.e., two years, five years, ten years), let them know it. They'll be able to keep you abreast of changes in the loan market, and they'll appreciate the repeat business.

How do you find a mortgage broker? Once you've chosen a realtor (see Chapter 9, Building a Team), he or she might recommend one to you. Or you can ask your friends if they have worked (with good results) with a broker in your area. As always, personal endorsements are a good place to start.

If you can't locate a broker through word-of-mouth, contact your local branch of the Mortgage Brokers Association for referrals.

What Lenders Look For

When you apply for a loan, lenders evaluate what they call the "Four Cs": collateral, cash, capacity and credit.

Collateral refers to the property itself, which in the U.S. is usually the sole collateral for the loan. An appraisal will be made to confirm that the property's value will support the amount of the loan.

Cash refers to the down payment. Lenders typically require a down payment of 10 to 20 percent or more of the property's sale price, along with closing costs.

Capacity refers to your income, debt, and cash reserves. Lenders will look at check stubs or tax returns, credit reports and bank statements to determine your ability to repay the loan.

Credit refers to your credit history: how you've handled your debts in the past. Your credit report will reveal the amounts and terms of past and present loans, how you've repaid them and are repaying them.

The Importance of Good Credit

The very first thing that lenders do after receiving your application is obtain a copy of your credit report. You can get a copy from them (after all, you're paying for it; the lender will usually tack on $30 to $75 for this service). But it's advisable to check out your credit report before you approach a lender. If there's an error or any negative information, then you can rectify it—or explain it—before you apply for a loan.

The Fair Credit Reporting Act authorizes you to obtain a copy of your credit report from any credit reporting agency for a reasonable charge. If you have been denied credit, disclosure is free within 30 days from the agency that provided your data to the lender. Generally, the letter that declined credit will list the reporting agency and provide an address to which you can send your request.

PAUSE: CREDIT REPORTING SERVICES

You may want to consider using a service that provides information from all three credit reporting bureaus: Equifax, Experian and Trans-Union. Discover Card offers Profile Protect to its cardholders for a monthly fee of $5.99. Profile Protect is a comprehensive report that compiles data from all three bureaus and provides an 800 number help-line for dealing with reporting inaccuracies.

However, it's a good idea to keep abreast of any changes to your credit report, and monitor it regularly. As an investor, keeping your credit in good standing is very important: it can make the difference between getting a loan or being denied, and will affect the interest rate and down payment of any loan you're offered. Those with higher credit ratings will be offered lower rates and more favorable loans. Your credit report plays an important part in your success with lenders.

What's On Your Credit Report?

Your credit report will list:

- Your name, date of birth, and Social Security Number;
- Your present and former addresses;
- Present and former employment;
- Public records on file: judgements, tax liens, and bankruptcies;
- Account information: mortgage(s) car loan(s), student or other loans, with payment histories, outstanding balances and credit limits;
- List of companies that have requested your credit report in the past six months.

Mistakes do occur and most often they're not in your favor. As you review your credit report, you should carefully check these items:

- Is your name, address, date of birth and Social Security number correct?
- Do all the accounts listed belong to you?
- Are all the accounts listed accurately?

- Has all negative information been deleted after seven years? (Chapter 7 bankruptcy is removed after 10 years.)
- Do you recognize all listed inquiries?

Correcting Errors and Bad Credit

If you discover inaccurate information on your credit report, you must write to the credit bureau responsible, and explain why the information is not correct. Under the Fair Credit Reporting Act, the credit bureau must investigate the matter, and correct any information it finds is not reported accurately. Information that cannot be verified should be deleted.

If you disagree with the results of the credit bureau's investigation, you are entitled to write a brief dispute statement that, at your request, will be included in future credit reports.

If the negative information on your credit report is true, make sure it is removed as soon as legally possible. In the meantime, do your utmost to improve your rating by paying your bills on time.

The Loan Application Checklist

Whether you're working on your own or with a broker, you'll need to collect a number of documents required for your loan application.

Income: W-2 forms or recent pay stubs. If you're self-employed, you may need to show tax returns for the previous two years.

Assets: Checking and savings account statements for the previous two to three months; real estate owned; automobile titles; list of savings bonds, stocks or investments and their current market value.

Debts: Most recent mortgage statement; copies of alimony or child support payments. Most information about your credit card debt, car loans or other loans will be gleaned from the lender's copy of your credit report, although they may ask you to provide additional documents such as credit card bills for the previous few months.

Information about the property: Copy of the purchase contract, cancelled deposit check.

Each lender has its own documentation requirements. To save time, call ahead and ask which supporting documents are necessary to complete the loan application.

Create a Loan Application File

Once you've rifled your desk drawers, file cabinets and shoe boxes for all the documents listed above, make copies of everything and create a separate file folder so that they'll be handy the next time you apply for a loan.

Into this file you may also want to add credit report updates, correspondence regarding errors on your credit reports, confirmation letters for the closing of a credit card account or personal loan, and documents regarding changes in marital status.

If you have all of the supporting materials for your loan application at hand, you'll find that the process of getting a loan is much less stressful.

REPLAY

When interest rates are low, 30-year fixed-rate loans are an investor's best choice.

Consider an ARM or hybrid mortgage when interest rates are high (above 8.5%).

The true cost of a loan, or APR, includes the interest rate, points and fees. Compare the Good Faith Estimates of several lenders.

Leveraging your investment with a 10% down payment and PMI means less cash out-of-pocket.

Mortgage brokers have access to hundreds of lenders, and can save you time and money.

Obtain a copy of your credit report and correct errors or bad credit before you shop for a loan.

Create a loan application file.

8

WORKING WITH FACILITATORS

YOU'VE GOT CASH AND YOU'RE READY TO INVEST—NOW what? If you're very busy, looking for the right property—and the right market, the right realtor, the right lender and the right property manager etc., etc.—may be too time-consuming. Happily, there's another option. You can work with a real estate facilitator.

What is a Real Estate Facilitator?

A real estate facilitator coordinates real estate investments for private investors. Generally, they don't own the properties they sell, but facilitate the transaction between buyer and seller. For a fee, facilitators can handle the process every step of the way: they research the best markets, coordinate a network of real estate professionals, locate property, negotiate the purchase price, arrange financing, expedite the paperwork and set up the property management.

One of the benefits to working with a facilitator is that you can find properties simply by going to their office and looking at spec sheets, or offers, of the houses they have for sale. They may also be able to mail or fax the offers to you. A facilitator's offer should have most of the information you'll need to make a decision about the property's investment value: a photograph of the house, its location, size (number of bedrooms, bathrooms, and square footage), price, and monthly rental rate. They will also have information about the city and neighborhood, including schools and shopping.

A facilitator will do the initial legwork for you, and will expedite the purchasing process by putting you in contact with tested realtors, lenders and escrow companies. Once you've bought the property, the facilitator will set you up with a property manager who will rent and maintain your property for you.

A good facilitating company will not only save time, but offers a support system that can help you throughout the life of your investment. When you invest through a facilitator, you benefit from being part of a large group of investors who have influence with realtors and property managers.

Working with a facilitator may mean the difference between investing and not investing. If you have little time to look for properties, I suggest that you contact a facilitator in your area.

Features of a Good Facilitating Company

As in all businesses, some facilitators are good—and some aren't so good. You'll want to make sure that you're working with a stable, responsible firm that's offering quality investment properties.

What to Look For

You should be able to find a facilitator in the yellow pages, or in your local newspaper. My company, ICG, offers free lectures that are listed in the "events" column in the real estate section. Going to a lecture is a good way to learn about the facilitator and the kinds of properties in which they specialize.

Of course, you can also call and ask them to send information about the company and a representative sample of their investment offers. Some things to look for include:

- In business for at least five years
- Offers quality properties in good markets
- Has references available
- Is listed with the Better Business Bureau and the local Chamber of Commerce
- Has network of reputable realtors and property managers that they work with on a continuing basis
- Professional, helpful, always available to answer questions
- On-going support before, during, and after your home purchase
- No high-pressure sales tactics

What to Look Out For

There are a few red-flags you should be aware of when considering facilitating firms. If you come across any one of the items below, say sayonara and keep looking.

- New company with no track record
- Offers low-quality properties in marginal areas
- Make unsubstantiated or unusually high claims of investment profitability
- No or very few references available
- Not listed with BBB or Chamber of Commerce
- High-pressure tactics; the sense that they're just out to make a sale
- Not available to answer your questions
- Encourages you to make false claims on loan applications or to defraud lenders

Important Questions to Ask a Facilitator

How long have you been in the real estate facilitating business?

A facilitator that's been in business for less than five years will not have proven experience or data on the long-term profitability of its investment properties.

How many properties have you bought?

Generally, the more the better. Facilitators who have the experience that comes from making many deals will usually have a solid network of other professionals that they work with, and will be more able to anticipate and deal with any problems that may arise.

How many clients have you worked with?

The more, the better generally goes for the number of clients, too…unless you feel that the facilitator is not servicing their clients well.

Can you furnish references?

If a facilitator cannot furnish references from satisfied clients, you will not want to do business with them. It's a big red flag.

Which markets do you buy in?

Now that you know the five essential criteria of a good investment market, you should be able to determine if the facilitator is working within markets in which you want to invest. The facilitator should be able to answer all your questions about demographics and neighborhoods: rental statistics, job market, schools, crime rate, etc. If they haven't done thorough research, then steer clear.

What kind of properties do you offer?

Do they offer single family homes or other types of property? A facilitator that specializes in apartment buildings or commercial property might not be the right one for you.

Can you help me plan my investment strategy and my future?

A good real estate facilitating company is more than just a liaison: it's a company with expertise in the real estate investing field. Do they offer this expertise as a part of their service? Will they help you make decisions about what's right for you? Will they help you look for investment homes that suit your needs, your budget and your goals?

Can you arrange financing, insurance, inspections, escrow and property management?

Precisely what services are they offering? Do they simply locate the property, or do they facilitate the entire process of purchasing and renting the property?

Will you be available to answer my questions even after I buy property?

Good real estate facilitators have an on-going relationship with their clients. They're available before, during and after the sale to help with all questions or concerns.

Will you help me if I have a disagreement with the property manager?

Because facilitators bring numerous clients to the property managers they work with, they should be willing to use this clout on your behalf.

What is your fee or commission?

The average facilitating fee amounts to 2% of the property's purchase price. If it's much higher than that, you may try negotiating a lower fee. If it's substantially lower, make sure that the company is offering all the services you need.

Can your fee be added to the price of the property and financed?

You should have the option to include the facilitator's fee in the mortgage. They're paid directly out of the home loan.

Do you have a service that will handle my investment on a monthly basis? What is your fee for this?

If you don't want to be bothered with the accounting tasks of your investment home, the facilitator may have a program that will handle this for you.

Examples of a Facilitator's Investment Offers

Following are two typical single family homes offered by my company, ICG. Each property has a "spec sheet" which provides a summary of the most important information you'll need when considering an investment property.

Along with a photograph of the property is a descriptive paragraph that lists its special features and upgrades. At top, you'll find the property's address, selling price, and the amount of the first mortgage (based on an investor loan with 10% down). In addition, the property's age, square footage, and configuration (i.e., 3 bedroom, 2 bath), are listed.

To the right of the photograph is a breakdown of monthly expense and income: principal and interest payment, PMI, taxes, insurance, property management fee, homeowner's association fee (if applicable), and the monthly rental rate. Also indicated are the estimated monthly cash flow figures.

A "spec sheet" should never be considered a substitute for actually inspecting the property, but it will give you an indication of the types of properties available from the facilitator.

When I work with new clients, I always encourage them to take a trip to see the properties before they buy. They are met at the airport by one of the realtors I work with, who then takes them on a tour of available homes. They also meet with the property managers. This way, they know beyond doubt that we're offering quality homes, and that we have a network of professionals with whom they can work on a continuing basis.

After a client has purchased a few homes, they seldom feel the need to make the journey to look at new investment properties. Often, they'll ask us to fax or mail spec sheets showing available properties and will choose another property based on price and location. They know that their next investment with us will be as good as, if not better than, their first. In this way, a real estate facilitator can make real estate investing as easy as trading stocks, or buying a CD!

Address	Price:	1st MTG.	
Parkwood Villages	$117,500	$105,561*	PITI
Mesa, Arizona	New Conventional Loan	7.875% Fixed	$947
	*Based on 10% down investor loan		

Features:
4 bedrooms, 2 baths
Fireplace, 2-car garage

Sq. ft.   1591

Monthly Expense/Income:

Principal/Interest	$ 765
PMI	$ 79
Tax (approx)	$ 78
Insurance	$ 25
Management	$ 63*
Homeowner's	$ 29
TOTAL:	$1039

Rental Rate:
$1050 to $1100

Cash Flow:
+$11 to +$61

*Plus 6% leasing fee, deducted from first month's rent.

Respected WOODSIDE HOMES is the builder of Parkside East Villages in Parkwood Ranch, Mesa. This development is conveniently located near freeways, shopping malls, restaurants and schools.

This 1591 square foot home is a single story home with distinctive Southwest-inspired architecture. This home has a durable concrete villa tile roof and low maintenance stucco exterior. Special features include decorative tan windows with front elevation grids, concealed air conditioning and heating units, brown masonry fence, coach lighted entry, embossed steel weather-resistent roll-up garage door, and wrought iron and cedar gates. The richly appointed kitchen boasts Euorpean style cabinets, Whirlpool oven and dishwasher, stainless steel double sink with disposal, water line to ice-maker, and electric dryer connections with vent. Energy saving features include an efficient ground mounted air conditioner, gas heating system, dual paned glazed tinted windows, and 40-gallon gas water heater. Other special extras include a 10-year warranty protection plan, smoke detectors, and dead bolts on ext. doors. The elegant baths have Moen faucets, fiberglass tub and showers.

<u>Upgrades included in this price are covered rear patio, front and back yard landscaping, garage door opener, and window blinds throughout.</u>

No comparables: New construction. Approximate down and closing are $15,400. ICG fee is included in the price.

Address	Price:	1st MTG.	
Waverly Woods	$128,900	$116,010*	PITI
Oviedo, FL	New Conventional Loan	7.875% Fixed	$1048
	*Based on 10% down investor loan		

Features:
4 bedrooms, 2 baths
Fireplace, 2-car garage

Sq. ft.   1900

Monthly Expense/Income:

PITI	$1048
PMI	$ 52
Management	$ 90
Homeowner's	$ 17
TOTAL:	$1207

Rental Rate:
$1225 to $1300

Cash Flow:
+18 to +$93

Waverly Woods is a great community of only 240 homes located in Oviedo, a lovely suburb of Orlando. Schools, shopping and recreation are all within a five-mile radius. Waverly Woods features many conservation lots, winding streets, tot lot, great location as well as excellent schools.

The "Brittany" is an elegant 1900 square foot, 4 bedroom, 2 bath home with 2-car garage and open patio. Special features include fungus resistant shingles, fully automatic irrigation system with St. Augustine grass, R-19 insulation in ceilings, fully equipped gourmet kitchen with range, microwave, dishwasher, dissposal, and separate breakfast nook. The master bath features a double vanity and large tiled shower with huge walk-in closet. Wall-to-wall carpet is included, with decorative no-wax vinyl floors installed in kitchen, nook, baths and foyer.

New construction. Earnest money deposit: $1,000. An additional deposit to make a total of 5% of the purchase price due at start of construction. Remainder of down payment and pre-paids due at closing.

Total down payment: $12,890. Closing costs and ICG fee paid by builder.

REPLAY

Real estate facilitators locate investment property, expedite the purchasing process, and arrange property management.

Good real estate facilitators offer quality properties in good locations.

Interview several facilitating firms; don't forget to check references.

A facilitator's "spec sheet" should include:
- Exterior photograph and address of property
- Style, age, size and price of property
- List of important features and upgrades
- Breakdown of monthly income and expenses
- Estimate of monthly cash flow

9

BUILDING A TEAM

HILARY CLINTON SAID IT "TAKES A VILLAGE" TO RAISE A CHILD, and you could almost say the same for purchasing real estate. Well, maybe not an entire village…but certainly a small burg.

A real estate transaction involves more than just you, the seller, and your respective realtors: it requires a whole group of real estate professionals, each of whom have a specific function to perform.

The Members of Your Team

Using the services of real estate professionals is essential for the busy investor. Each one of them offers expertise in specialized fields: real estate values, mortgages, title insurance, escrows, construction, and real estate law.

It isn't necessary for you to know the finer details of everything they do, but if you understand what's required of them in the course of your property purchase, you'll know if they're performing their job in a proper manner. Relying on their expertise will save you a great deal of time, and help you avoid mistakes.

Most real estate transactions involve all of these professionals:
- Real estate agent
- Real estate broker
- Lender
- Appraiser
- Escrow officer (or attorney, in certain states)
- Property inspector

Real Estate Agents and Brokers

Your realtor may be a real estate agent, and/or a real estate broker. What's the difference? A broker has a special state license and is ultimately responsible for making sure that the transaction is carried out to the letter of the law. All agents must be supervised by a broker; generally every office has a broker who oversees the deals that the agents make.

It isn't absolutely necessary for your agent to be a broker, although many good agents have a broker's license. Most agents are perfectly capable of taking care of your needs and handling the details of the sale. In most cases, you'll never meet the broker, unless something goes awry.

Lender

Whether you pre-qualify (apply for a loan before you've found a property), or find a lender during the course of buying the property, your purchase can't be completed until the financing is in place.

You can find a lender by using the services of a mortgage broker (see Chapter 7) or by referral from your real estate agent or facilitator.

Appraiser

An appraiser is an expert at assessing property values. He or she inspects the property in question and compares it to comparable properties, using size, location, condition, and recent sale prices to determine the market value of the home.

Typically, the property will be appraised after you have decided on a lender and qualified for a loan. An appraisal assures the lender that the house is worth an amount that justifies the amount of the mortgage. Lenders like to work with their own appraisers, and will arrange for the appraiser's inspection.

Escrow Officer

An escrow officer is a disinterested third party who works as a middle-man between the buyer and seller. Usually they work in conjunction with a title company. Title companies issue title insurance which insures that the title to the property was recorded correctly.

Once the real estate purchase agreement is negotiated and signed, the contract is handed over to an escrow officer who writes escrow instructions that include the sales price of the property, type of financing, how closing costs will be handled, and the dates on which the escrow opens and closes.

It's an escrow officer's job to ensure that both buyer and

seller are treated fairly, and that the terms of the real estate contract are met by both parties. Escrow officers prepare the necessary documents, conduct a title search, and make sure that the escrow closes on its stated date.

In some states, attorneys fill the role of the escrow officer. In this instance, usually both the buyer and seller have their own attorney.

Property Inspector

Property inspectors are hired by you, the buyer, to conduct a thorough inspection of the property before the close of escrow. They scrutinize the physical state of the property, examining roofs, electrical, heating and cooling systems, plumbing, foundations and every other aspect of the property for its condition.

It's important to have a professional inspector evaluate your property, even if it's new. They can alert you to structural defects or incipient problems that may affect the terms of the sale or your decision to buy the property.

Many reputable builders offer good warranties, which sometimes may obviate the need for an inspection. In a case like this, your realtor will conduct a "walk through" before the closing, at which he or she inspects the property themselves.

Your Realtor – the Quarterback of Your Team

A realtor is at the center of every real estate transaction. He or she functions as the liaison between you and all the other professionals required to facilitate a sale: real estate broker, seller's agent, lender, inspector, and escrow officer.

Technically, most realtors work for the seller as a sub-agent of the listing agent, but your realtor is also your representative who communicates your needs and requirements to the others involved in the sale. For this reason, it's important that you have a good rapport with your realtor, and that they understand your desires. Good realtors have good communication skills.

What Realtors Do

It's possible to buy real estate without a real estate agent but, in my opinion, it's like going into court without an attorney. Even the simplest real estate transaction requires a fundamental knowledge of local real estate laws and practices that's beyond the purview of the average investor. Real estate agents are, more often than not, worth every penny they earn. The time you spend with them represents just a small portion of the time they spend working for you.

What exactly do they do? To begin with, they continually look at properties in their area and have an extensive knowledge of the homes currently for sale and their market value. They can save time by sorting through the homes on the market and steer you towards the property that best fits your needs. Once you've selected a property, they'll make a comparative market analysis that compares the selling price of the property against recent comparable home sales. They'll negotiate with the seller's agent, prepare and present your offer, and draw up the purchase agreement. A real estate agent can help you find a lender, title company and escrow officer, and property inspector. Often, they'll be present at the inspection to ensure that the inspection is comprehensive.

Finding a Good Realtor

What should you look for when looking for a realtor? There are certain things that set the really good ones apart from the others.

Knowledge

Good realtors have extensive knowledge of the market in which they work. They've worked in the area for at least five years, and know the demographics of the city and the neighborhoods therein. They understand the dynamics of the market: median incomes, crime rates, major employers, and upcoming developments that may affect your investment, such as new construction, new schools, city or county projects, and zoning laws.

Good realtors know property values. This includes not only the current value of the property, but also the annual appreciation rate for properties in the area. They should also be familiar with rental rates, the ratio of homeowners to renters in the neighborhood in which you're looking, and vacancy statistics.

Experience

This may seem unfair to realtors who are just starting out, but I only recommend working with realtors who have been full-time realtors for at least five years.

As a busy investor, you need someone who's capable of handling any issue that may arise, and knows how to deal with it in a timely manner. A realtor with vast experience is going to be able to facilitate the buying process more quickly then a realtor with limited experience, and with better results.

Network

Good realtors don't work alone. They're in frequent contact with brokers, lenders, appraisers, inspectors, escrow officers and property managers. They've developed a network of other real estate professionals who assist them with real estate transactions, and they will use this network on your behalf. They will be able to refer you to a broker or lender who can arrange financing, title companies and escrow officers who can handle escrow, and property managers who can manage your investment.

How to Find the Right Realtor

The good news is that are many competent realtors out there who have the qualities listed above. The bad news is that there are many competent realtors out there who have the qualities listed above. You could conceivably spend a lot of time interviewing prospective agents and find it difficult to decide on just one.

Happily, there's another kind of expertise that, as an investor, is required from the realtor that you hire. You'll need a realtor who specializes in single family home investment properties.

These realtors are more rare, but they do exist. I work with numerous realtors who specialize in single family home investment properties in all the markets I've recommended.

Working with a realtor who understands the needs of real estate investors is crucial. They know what makes a good investment property. They know rental markets, rental rates, and work with investors and property managers on a daily basis.

Here's a relatively simple method for finding a good realtor who specializes in single family home investment properties.

Choose Your Market

Before you select a realtor, you've got to decide where you want to invest. As an example, let's assume you've chosen Houston, Texas.

Find Market Information

Next, you'll need to get information about your chosen area. Three primary sources are the Houston Sunday newspaper real estate section; the Houston Yellow Pages, and the Internet.

Book stores and newsstands often carry the Sunday newspapers of large cities; call around to see which stores in your area have the Houston paper, and have them set one aside for you. Procuring an out-of-town or out-of-state phone book is easily done with a call to your local telephone office; often the phone books are free, or have a minimal charge, and will be delivered to your home.

Internet access also provides you with a wealth of information on your chosen locality. Realtor.com and realestate.com are just two of many sites that offer realtor listings, property listings, and lots of general information.

Conduct Realtor Interviews

Pretty soon you'll have a list of realtors to contact. If you know the right questions to ask, you can get a very good feel for the experience, knowledge and general competence of a realtor just by talking with them on the phone.

Important Questions to Ask Realtors:

- How long have you been a realtor?
- How long have you worked in the area?
- Do you specialize in single family home investment properties?
- How many houses have you sold in the past year?
- How many people have you worked with?
- Can you provide references?
- Are you a broker, or do you work for a broker?
- If you work for a broker, does the broker take a percentage of your fee? If so, how much?
- Do you own investment property in the area? If so, what type? (SFH, apartments, etc.)
- Can you tell me where the good neighborhoods and schools are located?
- Are you familiar with the rental rates for single family homes in these neighborhoods?
- Can you tell me the ratio of owners to renters in these neighborhoods?
- Can you show me properties where the numbers work?
- Do you work with just one or a number of property man-

agers in the area?

- Do you recommend one property management company over the others, and for what reasons?

- Do you have time to meet with me when I visit your city?

- Do you have time to work with me?

The realtor you choose should be able to answer these questions to your satisfaction. He or she will be a full-time realtor, have at least five years' experience in the area, and will specialize in single family home investment properties. Your chosen realtor will have facilitated the sale of numerous investment properties within the past year, and be willing to provide references.

Once you've asked all these questions, you should know if the realtor is capable of handling your business. Then ask yourself how you feel about your conversation with them. Are they able to answer all your questions in detail? Is there any point on which you feel you've gotten less than a complete answer? Do you feel that you're able to communicate easily with them? Ideally, you'll feel a rapport with your realtor; when you meet the right one, you'll just "click."

REPLAY

Real estate transactions require the services of numerous real estate professionals.

A realtor is at the center of most real estate transactions, and is your liaison and representative.

Good realtors have knowledge, experience, and an established network.

Your chosen realtor must specialize in single family home investment properties.

Interview at least 3 or 4 realtors before making a decision.

10

SELECTING A PROPERTY

WHEN YOU FOLLOW THE "REMOTE CONTROLLED" METHOD, selecting an investment property is relatively easy. Reasonably priced, high quality investment homes in good neighborhoods are available in many cities in the U.S.

However, there are some key features you should keep in mind as you look for the right single family home. In this chapter, I'll cover the elements you should be thinking about as you and your realtor search for an investment property, along with tips on negotiating the purchase price, preparing a cash-flow analysis, and an overview of what happens during escrow and closing.

Location, Location, Location

I've said it before, and I'll say it again: buy where it makes sense to buy. You want a high quality property that will keep appreciating over a long term, which means buying only in

markets with the five essential criteria:
- Big City
- Good Rental Market Where the Numbers Work
- Not a Booming Market
- Low Median Price
- Sun Belt

Good Neighborhoods

A good location is, by definition, a good neighborhood. Good neighborhoods, like good markets, also have essential features.

The first recognizable feature of a good neighborhood is that it's composed of primarily single family homes: there should be very few or no duplexes, four-plexes, apartment buildings, or condominiums.

This may seem a bit stringent, but time and experience have shown me that buying single family homes in neighborhoods of composed of primarily single family homes is a much safer, sounder investment than buying homes in "mixed" neighborhoods. It promises the greatest rewards and the least trouble over the long-term.

Good neighborhoods also have good schools. They're the places in the city where most families want to live. They're safe, clean, and often have a homeowner's association that provides guidelines to help insure rising home values.

In good neighborhoods, most homes are owned by the people who live in them. "Pride of ownership" keeps the neighborhood's property values high, and makes it a more stable, safe, and desirable place to live. This insures the value of your rental property, and keep its value and rental rate rising over the years. Even when I purchase numerous homes in the same area, I make sure that I don't create too many rentals in one neighborhood.

Good neighborhoods are also distinctive for what they don't have. Good neighborhoods will have easy access to main streets and freeways, but they won't be too close to them. Good neighborhoods won't be near high-power lines, public utility plants, sewage treatment plants, or public dumps. Good neighborhoods should be near good schools, but not next to them.

PAUSE: 10 Main Features of a Good Neighborhood

Safe
Good schools
Convenient shopping
Majority of homes owned by residents
Composed primarily of single family homes
Near freeway, but not next to it
Near good schools, but not next to them
NOT near a busy street
NOT near high-power lines
NOT near sewage treatment plant or public dump

Looking at Properties

Once you've chosen a market, and selected the neighborhood(s) where you want to invest, you'll begin looking at properties on an individual basis. Sometimes investors—especially first-timers—get a little "hung up" at this juncture, because they use the same standards for a rental property as they would for a property they might live in.

When taken to the extreme, this can be a mistake. There's nothing wrong with liking the property you purchase, and occasionally, when two properties are essentially the same, a choice will be made on aesthetics alone. Generally, however, it's best to set aside your particular likes and dislikes regarding architecture, interior design and landscaping. Most renters won't make their decision based on whether the house is Spanish-style or traditional, the carpet is tan or taupe, or whether there are roses or daisies in the garden—and neither should you. Your investment property will be a successful rental primarily because of three things:

- **Right location**
- **Right size**
- **Right price**

And those are the things that you, as an investor, should look for, too. Of course, I'm assuming that you're looking only at quality homes in good condition. When you invest in a quality home in the right location (good neighborhood) that's the right size (three bedrooms and two baths minimum), and rents for the right price (in line with comparable rentals in the same area), then you've just purchased a successful rental, regardless of whether you think the bathroom wallpaper's a bit old fashioned, or wish the master bedroom was bigger.

I generally recommend that new investors steer clear of homes with swimming pools. Although they do add value to the property and make it attractive to the tenant, I believe that the drawbacks associated with swimming pools outweigh the benefits. Swimming pools are a danger to families with small children. They require a lot of maintenance and, in some states, require special fencing. This adds to your expenses and increases your liability.

PAUSE: The Important Features of a Winning Rental

Quality home in good neighborhood
Near good schools
3 bedroom, 2 bath minimum
Attached, 2-car garage
Well-tended, low-maintenance yard
Fenced backyard
No swimming pool
Easy access to good shopping
Near major employers

The Rule of Conformity: When "Average" is Good

If you're not looking for any extra-special features, then, what should you look for?

What you really want is an average house in a good neighborhood full of good homes. The rule of conformity means that to get the most value from your property, it should conform to the standards set by the majority of homes in the neighborhood.

Your investment property should be similar in style, size, condition and age to the houses that surround it. Furthermore, it should similar in price; ideally, the purchase price will approximate—or be lower than—the median price for the area.

The Benefits of New Homes

Buying a brand-new home—or one that's about to be built—offers a number of nifty advantages for investors.

The first is, of course, the house is new and everything is (or should be) in perfect condition. If there are any flaws, they'll be repaired under the homebuilder's warranty. You won't have to worry about repairs and refurbishments for at least the first few years. There's no need to paint, put in new wallpaper or new carpet. For busy investors, new homes are a godsend.

The second is that, because you're buying the house knowing that it will be a rental property, you can select the floor coverings, finishes, and appliances that will work best in a rental home. You'll want to choose neutral colors and durable, but not pricey, floor coverings, and appliances that can withstand the wear and tear of tenant turnover. Keeping an eye toward utility, not cosmetic beauty, will keep your initial costs down and minimize future replacement costs.

You can also choose a low-maintenance landscaping style. In Sun Belt areas this often means using drought-resistant plants and a drip system. Tenants aren't always avid gardeners, and a low-maintenance yard will reduce the need for a landscape service, while keeping the yard attractive.

A third bonus is that you can negotiate with builders for added amenities. Often the price of new homes is fixed, but builders are willing to offer upgrades such as a tile entry or backyard landscaping at no extra cost. Also, builders are often more willing than private owners to structure a deal that benefits you.

The fourth, and perhaps most intriguing benefit, is that you can actually earn equity before you've closed escrow. How is this possible? Purchasing a new home occurs in two stages. In the first stage, you sign a contract with the builder and make an earnest money deposit of a few thousand dollars. You don't have to come up with the down payment until the house is completed, usually four to six months later. In the Sun Belt regions we've discussed, more often than not the property value rises between signing and closing. Many investors have purchased homes that have appreciated two to four percent in less than six months.

Very importantly, new homes define the concept of a good neighborhood. Where new homes are built, new schools and shopping centers are built, too. More and more, new home developments are part of a master-planned community with amenities such as parks, swimming pools, softball and soccer fields, and walking trails: just the kind of place where most families want to live.

Analyzing Your Potential Investment Property, or Making the Numbers Work

Before you make an offer on a house, you'll want to be certain that it will be a good investment. You do this by preparing a cash-flow analysis of the property, or what I call "making the numbers work."

Before you can analyze the property, you must ask your realtor or property manager to supply you with answers to these questions:

- What will the property rent for?
- Is there a homeowner's association in the neighborhood? What are the monthly dues?
- What is the fee for property management?
- What is the annual property tax for this property?

Essentially, a cash-flow analysis is a summary of monthly income (rent) minus monthly expenses (mortgage principal and interest, PMI, taxes, insurance, property management fees and homeowner's association dues).

Following are two examples taken from actual properties in the Phoenix area.

PROPERTY #1

Sale Price:	$130,000
Down payment and closing costs:	$ 15,000
Mortgage:	$117,000 (30 yr. fixed @ 8%)

Monthly rent rate:	$1125 to $1200

Principal and interest:	$858
Taxes:	$ 95
Insurance:	$ 25
PMI:	$ 82
Prop. Management:	$ 50
Homeowner's Assoc.:	$ 30

TOTAL:	$1140

Monthly cash flow:	-$15 to +$60

PROPERTY #2

Sale Price: $146,500
Down payment
and closing costs: $ 17,000
Mortgage: $131,850 (30 yr. fixed @ 8%)

Monthly rent rate: $1300 to $1350

Principal and interest: $968
Taxes: $105
Insurance: $ 25
PMI: $ 93
Prop. Management: $ 75
Homeowner's Assoc.: $ 30

TOTAL: $1296

Monthly cash flow: +$4 to +$54

As you can see from the examples, the cash-flow analyses for the two properties show a slight negative to slight positive monthly cash flow. Does this mean the numbers don't work?

On the contrary. The properties analyzed above are examples of investments that do work. Remember three things:

- **These properties have been leveraged as much as possible, with low down payments of 10%.** Using a larger down payment will reduce the size of the mortgage, the monthly principal and interest payment, and delete the PMI, which will produce a higher positive cash–flow.

- **Even if you use a 10% down payment, the PMI will probably drop off in a few years.** Rents will likely go up and, if the mortgage is fixed, cash flow will improve.

- **Tax benefits have not been factored in.**

Analyzing Your After-Tax Cash Flow

Although the Tax Reform Act of 1986 imposed stricter limitations on losses from real estate investments, you can still benefit from the favored status the government bestows on real estate investors. Along with deductions for repairs, travel and other expenses incurred from your rental activities, you can take a just-for-tax-purposes loss against your property.

Cost Recovery, or Depreciation

Depreciation, also known as cost recovery, is a deduction the government allows you to take to recover the cost of investment property that has a life beyond the tax year. For residential rental property, depreciation is deducted over a 27.5 year period.

However, only a certain portion of the property's cost can be depreciated. The amount that can be depreciated is known as the improvement value, which is the cost of the property minus the value of the land.

To determine the improvement value of the property, you'll need to consult your tax preparer, realtor or appraiser. Although home building costs are relatively consistent throughout the country, the price of land varies greatly from region to region. Real estate prices are often determined by land values. In states such as California, it's the value of the land that has driven real estate prices so high.

This brings me to another reason why I choose to buy investment property in the Sun Belt. The cost of land is relatively low, so the improvement value is high in relation to the total cost of the property.

For example, let's compare two similar homes, one in California and one in Arizona. An average three-bedroom, two-bath house in the San Francisco Bay Area costs $350,000. Land in the Bay Area is so expensive that the improvement value of the property is around $175,000, or only 50% of the total price. In Phoenix, an average three-bedroom, two-bath house sells for $135,000. Because land in Phoenix is less expensive than in the Bay Area, the Phoenix property has an improvement value of $108,000, or 80% of the total price.

Land in the San Francisco Bay Area is expensive because the Bay Area is perceived as a great place to live, and so the demand for housing exceeds the supply. But if this perception of the Bay Area as great place to live were to change—for instance, if there was a massive earthquake—then the value of the land would decrease, and very possibly cause a significant decrease in home values.

In other words, there's a lot of "air" between the perceived value of the Bay Area property and its intrinsic value. That makes it much more vulnerable to economic and other fluctuations. Whereas the property in Phoenix is much less volatile, because it has a greater intrinsic value, and a lot less "air" between its perceived value and its intrinsic value.

When the improvement value of a property is high, the property is less vulnerable to economic downturns. It also means that you will be able to depreciate a greater percentage of the property's overall value, and that your depreciation deduction will go further toward offsetting your tax liability. In markets where land is at a premium, your depreciation deduction will not benefit you as much as in markets where the cost of land is lower.

How Depreciation is Calculated

Here's an example of how depreciation, or cost recovery, is calculated. Let's assume that Property #1 has an improvement value of $100,000. The deduction on a residential investment property with an improvement value of $100,000 is $3636 per year, for 27.5 years. Let's also assume that the property rents at the low end, for $1125 per month, and produces an annual negative cash flow of $180. When you add your depreciation deduction of $3636, you can claim a loss of $3816. If you're in the 28% tax bracket, that's a tax savings of $1068— and a positive monthly cash flow of $89.

Property #2 has an improvement value of $115,000 and rents for $1350 a month, producing a positive annual cash-flow of $648. On a property with an improvement value of $115,000, the depreciation deduction is $4181. After subtracting your profits ($648), you still have a tax loss of $3533. If you're in the 28% tax bracket, this leads to a tax savings of $989. When you add the profits and tax savings together, you've made a total of $1637 for the year; that's a positive cash flow of $136 per month.

Note that these figures are applicable only for the first one to three years of your investment. As rental prices rise, your positive cash-flow will increase, yet the depreciation deduction will help keep your taxable profits low.

Although I think the two properties analyzed above are perfect examples of good investments, keep in mind that using high leverage and a "break-even" scenario isn't the only way to structure your investment. By putting more money down, you won't have to pay PMI, you'll have a higher positive cash-flow, and you can use the profit to pay off the loan sooner. Remember, though, that positive cash-flow is not the Holy Grail of real estate investing. It's also important to look at how much money comes out of your pocket to make the investment.

For instance, if the cash-flow analysis of a potential property reveals that, with only 10% down, you'll have a $150 per month negative cash-flow before taxes, ask yourself which is better: to shell out another $10,000 for a 20% down payment, or to pay $150 a month until the rent rises? As long as the negative cash-flow is reasonable and doesn't overtax your budget, it makes more economic sense to reserve your capital and pay the difference between rental income and expenses. In addition, the $150 a month loss is tax-deductible; the down-payment isn't.

As you can see, properties with a slight negative cash-flow can still be good investments.

Making an Offer: Tips on Negotiating a Purchase Price

I like a good deal as much as the next guy. But when it comes to buying a single family home investment property, a good deal usually means paying fair market value, or, if things go well, slightly less. In this case, it doesn't mean getting a "steal."

When you buy a quality home in a quality neighborhood in a quality market, you aren't going to have as much "wiggle room" on the price as you will when buying low quality properties in bad markets. It's important to remember that you're investing in your future, not trying to "make a killing" overnight.

That said, there are things you can do to get a fair and reasonable price on an investment property. First, make sure that your realtor is cognizant of comparable sales in the neighborhood and knows the fair market value of the property. He or she should be able to counsel you on the best offer to make and, as long as it's close to the fair market value, you can consider it a good deal: "fair" means fair to both seller and buyer. Some real estate investors, however, insist on bidding under the seller's asking price simply because it makes them feel better about buying property if they feel they're getting a "deal."

While there's nothing wrong with doing this, you do take the chance that your offer will fall on deaf ears. If you've found a property that you think is a good investment, and it meets all the criteria, you might not want to take that chance.

Never forget that you're making a long-term investment. Don't blow it just because the seller won't drop the price $2000 or $3000. That money's going to be financed over 30 years, after all, and represents only $200 or $300 out of your pocket. Fifteen years into the future, when the property's worth twice what you paid for it, will you care if you paid $130,000 or $133,000? Most likely you won't—you'll just be glad you bought it.

Negotiating with Builders

Buying new homes does offer some advantages when negotiating the purchase price. More than individual owners, new home builders are comfortable structuring a deal with a few bells and whistles. For instance, they're generally happy to cover all or part of the closing costs by adding it to the purchase price, which will cut down on the amount of cash you'll have to pay up front.

A good time to negotiate with home builders is near the end of the fiscal year, or when they're at the end of a subdivision. At all times, however, they are usually willing to offer amenity incentives: things that increase the value of the property but don't increase the price. For example, they may offer a better lot, backyard landscaping, appliances or upgraded carpet. Sometimes builders will entice you to use their lender, but you'll want to be cautious about this. In many cases the builder's lender will have higher loan fees than a lender you would find on your own. Be sure you check before committing yourself.

What Happens During Escrow and Closing

Once the offer is signed between you and the seller, the contract and your earnest money deposit are delivered to an escrow officer who will oversee the exchange of money and property.

Escrow officers work for escrow firms or title companies, and are disinterested third parties who guarantee that both you and the seller are treated fairly. They prepare documents related to the transfer of title, order a title search, and work with lenders for the transfer of funds. They're in charge of making sure that all documents are signed and delivered, and that the transfer of title is made public record.

After the escrow officer receives your contract, he or she will write a set of escrow instructions that is sent to you and the seller. The instructions include the date escrow is scheduled to close, and any contingencies, or conditions of sale, that affect the transaction.

Contingencies insure that you can cancel the sale if stated conditions are not met; for example, if the property inspection report reveals structural or other damage, if you don't qualify for a loan, or if the title search uncovers unexpected liens or judgements.

During escrow, you'll receive a preliminary title report that will show who currently owns the property, along with claims against the property such as mortgages, tax assessments, or income tax judgements. The current owner is required to clear the title of liens and judgements before the close of escrow.

Escrow is the time when you'll conduct a property inspection, and obtain homeowner's insurance for the property (in fact, your escrow officer will prompt you to get it—escrow can't close until you're properly insured). If your loan has not already been approved, you'll be working with the escrow officer and the lender to get your funding in place.

Once your loan is approved, the title is clear, and all contingencies to the sale have been resolved, escrow "closes"; that is, the lender sends funds to the escrow company for transfer to the seller, and the transfer of title is recorded in the County Recorder's office. You'll receive a final "settlement statement" that lists the money you deposited in escrow (your initial deposit, down payment and mortgage loan), and the funds paid out of escrow on your behalf (the total amount paid to the seller, loan fees, title fees, property inspection fees).

At all times during the escrow process, your realtor should be available to answer any questions or concerns that you have. They've been through the process many times, and should be in constant communication with your escrow officer. Good realtors can be extremely helpful with resolving issues between you and the seller, and can help the escrow proceedings move along efficiently.

REPLAY

Buy in markets with the 5 essential criteria:
- Big City
- Good Rental Market Where the Numbers Work
- Not a Booming Market
- Low Median Price
- Sun Belt

Good neighborhoods are composed primarily of single family homes.

Good neighborhoods have good schools, are safe, clean and convenient to shopping centers.

The location, size, and price of your investment home matter more than the aesthetics.

New homes have many benefits for investors.

Rely on your realtor to help with the escrow process.

11

LET THE PROS MANAGE IT: RENTING YOUR PROPERTY

Scenario number one: You've just purchased an investment property, and you decide to manage it yourself. First, you've got to find a tenant. You post a "For Rent" sign on the lawn, place advertisements in the local newspapers, and spend much more time answering phone calls than you anticipated. You meet with prospective tenants, make sure they've filled out the rental application completely, and spend more time checking their references and talking to former landlords. Once you've narrowed the field, you run credit checks through a credit reporting service at $25 a pop.

Finally, after a month or two, you've found a tenant. You sigh with relief, thinking that the hard part's over. But too often, for too many landlords, the work's just begun.

First, the water heater quits. Next, little Susie flushes her Barbie down the toilet, or little Jimmie decides to see what happens after he drops a half-dozen marbles in the kitchen sink and turns on the Disposal. A winter storm blows off a few roof tiles. The kids next door break a window playing baseball. A pipe bursts. The bathtub faucet leaks. The rain gutters need cleaning. A broken tile in the foyer must be replaced. The tree in the front yard needs a trim.

It's true that all homes need the occasional repair, and if you're already a homeowner, this list of troubles might not faze you. The difference between your own home and your rental property, however, is that repairs to your rental have to be taken care of immediately, regardless of when they occur (the worst things always seem to happen at three a.m., or while you're on vacation). You may not mind going without hot water for three days, but by law, your tenant is entitled to a hotel stay as long as the hot water or heat is non-functional.

Until you manage a rental property yourself, you might not realize how much of your time and effort is required to make these repairs. And I'm not talking about doing it yourself. Simply finding the necessary contractors, negotiating prices, and arranging dates and times convenient to both the contractor and the tenant takes a considerable amount of time. Then, of course, you've got to make sure the work was done properly.

If the rent payment is late, you'll have to deal with the tenant on an issue that is bound to be stressful to both of you. When the tenant moves out, it's up to you to determine the amount of the cleaning deposit refund: whether the tenant's toll on your property is the result of normal wear and tear, or if excessive wear will require you to withhold some of the deposit. This problem, more than any other, is what brings landlords and tenants together in small claims court. That's another big chunk of your time, not to mention the unpleasantness of it all.

And, of course, when your present tenant moves out, you'll have to start all over again...getting the property in move-in condition, advertising, taking phone calls, interviewing prospective tenants, and conducting background checks.

If you have time, patience, and a good sense of humor ("Please tell little Susie how sorry I am to hear that only Barbie's head survived the tragic accident") managing your investment properties might work for you. But I suspect that, like most of us, your life is already full to the bursting point. Does that mean you can't own investment property? Not at all. Which brings me to...

Scenario number two:

You've just purchased an investment home, and have hired a property management company that specializes in the management of single family residences. What happens next? Very, very little. At most, you'll approve the tenant they've chosen and sign the lease.

What about repairs? Late payments? Cleaning deposit refunds? The property manager is there to handle everything, from advertising the rental and screening tenants, to hiring contractors and overseeing the repair work...and more. You won't have to do much more than approve (or not approve) any repair expenses. You'll never get a phone call at three a.m., or while you're on vacation (unless you've specifically asked the property manager to contact you).

In most cases, when you hire a property manager, your investment will require only a little of your time via the occasional phone call. For me, there's no contest between the two scenarios. If you're busy, property management is the only way to go.

What Property Managers Do

A full-service property management company has four coordinating functions: people (tenant screening); financial (rent collection and disbursement, accounting services); construction (maintenance and repair); and legal (lease agreements, eviction proceedings). They are responsible for renting and managing your property in all its aspects, and will offer these services:

- Advertising and marketing
- Property showing
- Tenant screening, including credit checks and background checks
- Lease negotiation
- Rent collection
- Repair coordination and oversight
- Property inspection
- Monthly and annual accounting
- Lease renewal
- Tenant negotiation
- Eviction services

After you sign on with a property management company, they determine the monthly rental rate based on comparable rentals in the surrounding area. The property manager then advertises the rental, using all the means at their disposal, including newspaper advertising, signage, Web based advertising, and multiple listing services.

The property management company will show the property, collect tenant applications, conduct tenant interviews and credit checks, and review the rental history of potential tenants. They will offer recommendations on the best tenant for your property. After the lease agreement is signed between you and the tenant, the property management company will make sure that your rental property is in move-in condition.

Each month the property management company will collect rent from your tenant. The check will be deposited in a large trust account in which you, the property owner, have a separate account. You are paid by the property management company out of this trust account.

The property management company will keep you apprised of any necessary repairs and will coordinate the repairs by contacting tenants to arrange times for vendors or repairmen to come by. Often, property managers work with a select group of contractors with whom they've negotiated discount pricing.

The property manager understands the state and local landlord-tenant laws. This is extremely important if any problems arise with your tenant. A good property manager can help you stay out of small claims court and knows how to conduct a tenant eviction so that it's effective yet abides by state and local laws.

An important part of property management occurs when there's a tenant turnover. A difficult aspect of rental management is distinguishing normal wear and tear on a property from excess wear. The property manager knows how to tell the difference and how to determine the correct amount of the deposit refund. They can help you avoid any disputes over this issue, which is often a troublesome one for property owners.

Benefits to You, the Property Owner

Just as your stock portfolio or 401(k) is managed by someone who is familiar with the stock market, property managers are asset managers. They have vast experience working with many property owners and many tenants and can do much to promote the profitability of your property. They can also help you avoid the problems that sometimes accompany property ownership. When you use a property manager you don't have to screen tenants, collect rent, advertise or hire contractors. In addition, property managers can protect your anonymity, if you prefer being anonymous.

The primary benefit to using a property manager is that it saves you time. You don't have to be an active landlord, or learn the many skills involved in successfully managing your property (and too often novice real estate investors learn the hard way, through costly mistakes). The monthly and annual statements prepared by the property management company will make your bookkeeping tasks much easier, with your income and expenses already calculated, ready to be entered into your tax return.

Cost of Property Management

Property management companies charge a percentage, usually somewhere between six percent and nine percent, of the gross rent collected. For a house that rents for $1000 a month, the property management fee would be between $60 to $90 per month. Their fee is deducted monthly from the rental income, before a check is issued to the property owner.

Selecting a Property Management Company

You can find property management companies in the Yellow Pages under "Real Estate Management." Another good source is the National Association of Residential Property Managers (NARPM) Web site at www.narpm.org, which offers a search feature of property managers by region. This association of 1300 property managers requires members to have a tested level of professional skill and to abide by a code of ethics.

Narrow the field first by selecting only full-time property management firms. This means no part-time or side-line property managers; often real estate offices or other real estate professionals will advertise themselves as property managers, sometimes offering a cut-rate fee. As in most things in life, you pay for what you get, and slip-shod management can be worse than no management at all. What you want is a management company that will be available 24 hours a day, if necessary, and one that will manage your asset on every front, from showing and renting to repairs and maintenance.

Important Questions to Ask Potential Property Managers

How long have you been in business?

The longer, the better, of course. Experience counts.

Are you a member of any professional associations?

The National Association of Residential Property Managers (NARPM) and the Property Managers Association (PMA) are two professional associations that require management companies to abide by professional standards and practices.

Do you specialize in residential properties?

You want a management company that either specializes or deals only in residential management. Companies that specialize in commercial property management (office buildings, etc.) may not understand your or your tenant's needs.

Do you work weekends?

A good property management company is available to oversee your property 24 hours a day, seven days a week. Don't accept anything less!

How many properties do you currently manage? What is the total number of properties you've managed?

As above, experience counts…just be sure they have the staff necessary to handle their clientele.

Are these properties in the same area or neighborhood as my property?

Knowledge of the neighborhood in which your property is located is preferred. This means that the property management company will know the type and age of your property, and comparable rentals. They'll also be familiar with the neighborhood homeowner's association.

Can you supply references?

Ask for the names and numbers of a few other property owners who have properties similar to yours. Don't hesitate to call them and ask if they've been satisfied by the service they've received from the management company.

Which services do you offer?

Make sure that the management company offers all of the services listed above.

What is your fee?

Somewhere between six and nine percent of the gross rent collected is the standard throughout the industry, as is a fee for leasing. Keep in mind that you may be able to negotiate a lower fee than what the management company is asking for, especially if you have multiple properties.

Do you charge a leasing fee?

A leasing fee is standard, and is usually for an amount equal to one-half to one month's rent. It covers advertising costs, fees to other managers for bringing in tenants from an MLS listing, credit checks and other expenses associated with qualifying tenants, showing the property, etc.

Do you have an additional fee for lease renewal?

In most cases, there is not a separate fee for lease renewal, if the leasing fee has been paid. Some managers do charge a small fee.

How do you advertise and market the properties you manage?

Excellent marketing skills are crucial to the profitability of your property. The management company you choose should advertise and market your property on multiple fronts: through the Multiple Listing Service, newspaper advertising, and, if available, Web based advertising.

What is the average time for renting a new property?

The time it takes to rent your property often depends on the amount of rental activity in the market where your property is located. In the markets which I've mentioned earlier in the book (Phoenix, Orlando, etc.), residential properties can usually be rented in one to two months. If the management company quotes a longer period than that, find out why.

What is the average time to "turn-around" a property: cleaning, repairs, new tenant?

You're hiring a management company to help keep your property profitable. Be certain they have all the vendors (painters, carpet cleaners, etc.) necessary to keep turn-around time to a minimum.

How often do you check on the property?

The property manager who is assigned to your property should conduct periodic drive-by checks. Find out how often they intend to make a drive-by inspection and what they look for.

Which vendors and contractors do you work with?

The management company should be able to provide you with a list of their vendors and contractors: appliance dealers, plumbers, carpenters, landscape services, etc. Make certain that the contractors are licensed and bonded.

How do you handle late payments?

Generally, management companies collect rent on a specified day each month, the first or the fifth. If a rent payment is late, they will issue a late notice. You'll want to know if they have any special techniques or skills for dealing with late-paying tenants.

Have you ever evicted tenants? What is your procedure? What is the cost to the owner?

Evictions, of course, must follow the laws set down by the state in which your property is located. Ask the management company to explain the local eviction laws, and whether they have a legal department or attorney on retainer who will handle it.

Do you issue monthly and annual statements?

Accountability is an important feature of a good property management company. They should have computerized accounting which issues a monthly statement with income (rent payments) and expenses (management fee, repairs) clearly stated. In addition, an annual statement should reflect all monthly statements and any tax information you need for your tax return.

Once you've asked all these questions, you should know if the property management company is capable of taking care of all your needs. Then ask yourself how you feel about your conversation with them. Are they able to answer all your questions in detail? Is there any point on which you feel you've gotten less than a complete answer? How are their communications skills? One of the primary jobs of a property manager is dealing with tenants, and good communication is requisite.

How to Minimize Vacancies: Tips on Attracting and Keeping Good Tenants

First of all, what's a good tenant? The bottom line is, of course, one who pays the rent on time. Ask a few property owners and you'll come up with a wish list of other qualities: stays in the rental for years, never complains, keeps your property looking like a showplace, is an avid gardener, doesn't mind making minor repairs, is always available to open the house up for contractors, doesn't open an auto repair business on the front lawn or start fires in the kitchen.

This, however, is a dream tenant, and those are hard to come by. Happily, when you've got a good property manager, your peace of mind doesn't have to rely on an elusive dream tenant. A good tenant—one who's responsible and reasonable—will do just fine. Here are a few pointers that will help you attract good tenants, and keep them.

Keep your property in excellent shape functionally and aesthetically.

When your investment property shows pride of ownership—clean, with a well-tended yard, fresh paint and spotless floor coverings—you're going to attract a better class of tenant.

Allow children and pets.

Remember, you're investing in single family residences. Families have children. Families have pets. Yes, Fido and Fluffy might do a little damage to the carpets or the yard, but it's fixable. What's more important is that your tenant remains in the house for at least two or three years. Families with children and pets tend to settle in and stay awhile, especially if your property is located in a good neighborhood, with good schools. A few square feet of carpet is much less costly than vacancies and tenant turnover.

Create low-maintenance yards or hire a gardening service.

No doubt your tenant is as busy as you are. And, like most of us, they probably don't have the time or the inclination to be out in the yard mowing, watering, and pruning every weekend.

Do yourself and them a favor by creating an easy–care yard with a drip system, or hiring a landscape service. In Sun Belt areas, desert landscaping is a good bet. Desert landscaping usually consists of indigenous plants that need little or no water along with colored rocks and sand. It's attractive, with zero to low maintenance. Your tenants will appreciate coming home every night to a house with an attractive yard, and you'll know, without a doubt, that your property will always have curb-side appeal—and will look good for the next tenant.

Be respectful.

Your investment may be your property, but it's your tenant's home. They deserve a landlord who respects their privacy, is cognizant of their needs, and responsive to their problems. This doesn't mean you have to be available to them day and night, but it is up to you to make sure their problems are being addressed promptly by the management company.

The Dos and Don'ts of Repairs and Renovations

The most common mistake I see among property owners, especially those who own single family homes, is the tendency to impose their own aesthetic standards and values on their rental property.

For example, an investor from California purchased a single family home in Arizona. In Arizona, electric kitchens are common. In California, it's the opposite: gas stoves are the norm, and considered more desirable than electric.

This investor decided that, to make his property more appealing, he would rip out the electric kitchen and install gas appliances. Three months and thousands of dollars later, he'd changed a perfectly good kitchen into one that suited his needs.

Did the house rent faster? No. Was he able to charge a higher rent? No. All the owner had done was reduce the profitability of his investment—and, in fact, the kitchen looked worse than before.

Over-improvement can be as detrimental to your investment's bottom-line as neglecting the property. Repairs and renovations to rental properties should be based upon functionality, not aesthetics. Of course you want your investment home to look nice, but it doesn't have to conform to your idea of beauty, or even convenience. Save that for the home you live in.

Good rental properties adhere to the standards set by similar rental properties in the surrounding neighborhood.

Necessary Repairs

When you buy a quality home in a good neighborhood, you won't have to worry much about major repairs. Houses less than 15 years old seldom need new foundations, new heating systems or extensive re-plumbing. The lack of major repair work is one of the many reasons why I recommend buying brand-new, high-quality properties. No matter what the age of your property, however, you'll want to make certain that all the items listed below are in perfect working order. Keep in mind, however, that you'll have a team—your property management company—to keep abreast of all this.

Roof

Composition roofs generally need to be replaced every 15-20 years. In Arizona, many newer homes have tile roofs, which last a lot longer.

Foundation

Bad foundations cause stress on the structure, which leads to all kinds of problems: interior cracks, stuck doors and windows, roof problems, etc.

Garage Door

Whether it's manual or automatic, the garage door should open smoothly and easily. An automatic garage door is always preferable.

Driveway

Cracks in the driveway are unsightly, and are a detriment to the "curb-side" appeal of your home. Small cracks left untended have a tendency to become larger; weeds can grow in the cracks, forcing the concrete farther apart. It's best to take care of them early on.

Fences

Many states have fencing laws that must be adhered to. Having a broken or incomplete fence around your property can lead to lawsuits.

Heating and Cooling Systems

Thermostats, furnaces, and air vents should all be checked periodically. Often, the local gas and electric company will do a free inspection of the property's heating and cooling system, relight extinguished pilot lights, and check carbon monoxide levels.

Plumbing

Toilets, tubs, and showers should have strong water pressure and good drainage. Problems with toilet flushing can often be repaired by replacing the parts inside the toilet tank, especially is it's a relatively new toilet. Hot water heaters have an average life of 20 years; an occasional "flush" (draining so the sediment in the bottom is cleaned out) can help keep them working efficiently. If your tenants have children, you may want to keep the hot water temperature set below 110 degrees, to prevent accidental scalding.

Electrical

All outlets and light fixtures should be functional. Large appliances such as refrigerators, washers, dryers, and dishwashers should have grounded 220 electrical hookups.

Fireplace

The flu inside the fireplace should open and close smoothly, and smoke should draw easily. Brick and mortar fireplaces should be inspected for cracks or damage. A fireplace cover, such as one with sliding glass doors, reduces the possibility of accidents, fire, and also reduces the amount of smoke and soot that gets into the house.

Appliances

All appliances should be clean and work efficiently. They

don't have to be state-of-the-art, but should look relatively new. Inspect washer and dishwasher for proper drainage and leaking. The clothes dryer must have adequate ventilation; dryer lint build-up is a fire hazard.

Floor Coverings

All carpeting, linoleum and tile should be clean and in good condition, without stains, holes, tears, or cracks. You don't have to carpet the entire house just because there are problems in one room; usually you can find carpet that will closely match the existing carpet.

Doors and Windows

Doors should be level, and able to close tightly. Windows should be without cracks in panes or sashes, and should open easily.

Window Treatments

I usually have mini-blinds installed on the windows of my rental properties. They're inexpensive, yet look good from the house exterior, and provide a consistent look throughout the house. Curtains tend to be more expensive, and more prone to wear and tear.

Smoke Alarms

Smoke alarms should be installed in each bedroom, the living room (especially if there's a fireplace), and in the kitchen. You may even want to add a small fire extinguisher in the kitchen, easily accessible in case someone's flambé gets out of hand. Smoke alarms should be checked periodically, and new batteries installed once a year. Check with your management company to make sure this is part of its oversight. Don't rely on your tenants to take care of this!

Security

Adequate security is as important to your tenant as it is to you. There should be deadbolts on both the front and back doors; sliding glass doors and windows should shut and lock securely.

Walls

Holes, cracks and water stains should be repaired. Marks or scratches can often be removed simply by cleaning, or paint touch-ups. Generally bedroom walls take the most abuse, especially if children live in the house. It's also common to paint before a new tenant moves in, unless the previous tenant was there for less than a year.

All the above are maintenance issues. Paying attention to them is important; keeping these things in good repair keeps your property functional, safe, and livable. When your property manager calls and tells you there's a problem with any of the above items, you need to listen. Ignoring the structural systems of your house will only make problems worse, and will often lead to unhappy owner-tenant relations.

On the other hand, you are not required to make cosmetic changes or upgrades to please your tenant. These would include new paint or carpet, when the current paint and carpet is in good condition; wallpaper, new appliances, microwave ovens, additional landscaping, bay windows, patio covers, etc. It will help you to know what is considered standard for other rentals in the area; your property manager can help with this. And, in fact, he or she can help you make decisions about your property that are good business decisions, and not based on personal taste.

REPLAY

Personally managing your property is time consuming.

Although you can choose to make all final decisions, a property management company can save you time, costly mistakes, and help keep your investment profitable.

Property management companies usually charge a fee of 6% to 9% of the gross rent collected, plus a leasing fee.

Conduct an in-depth interview with several property management companies before making your decision.

Check references.

Good tenants are attracted to good properties, and fair, responsible owners.

Cosmetic changes or upgrades to your property are not cost-effective.

12

BUILDING YOUR PORTFOLIO

ONE OF THE ADVANTAGES OF REAL ESTATE IS THE ABILITY TO leverage your initial investment into further investments, thereby increasing your net worth and income.

Your ultimate goal should be to purchase multiple properties. How many properties you purchase depends on your needs and goals. When you buy quality single family homes in good neighborhoods, and have them managed by professional property managers, the number of homes you can own is limited only by the capital at your disposal.

Setting Goals

Soon after you buy your first investment home—or even before—sit down with your spouse or significant other and discuss your life goals. If you don't have a significant other, you may want to confer with your CPA or tax advisor. There's something about talking about your goals that makes them more real, and forces you to look at the reality of your current situation. It's one thing to have a recurring fantasy of quitting your job and sailing around the world; but once you say it out loud, your partner's either going to point out the complete unfeasibility of the idea, or help create a plan to make it happen (hopefully, your spouse loves to sail, too). Talking about what you want from life will help you make decisions and commitments. The dreams that are never discussed are usually the ones that are never realized.

The first thing you should talk about is the age at which you want to retire. As with all long-term goals, this may change over the years; the important thing is to choose a number and set a goal. For most people, the golden age is still 65. Even if you believe that you'll never retire, choose a number. As you grow older, you'll realize how important is it to invest for your later years. After all, even multi-millionaires can continue to work, if they want to—the difference between them and most people is that they have a choice.

Next, consider the annual income you'll need after retirement. Remember, you only need to think in terms of today's dollars. If you were to retire today, how much income would you require each year? Finally, what financial hurdles do you face before retirement? Will you need to finance a college education, help provide for your parents' retirement, or would you like to start your own business? If you've already completed the steps in Chapter Six, you've got a good sense of your current financial picture, and have begun putting aside investment funds. Now's the time to decide when you want to reach your goals, and make a time-line for investing.

How to Estimate the Number of Properties You'll Need

Your retirement income will come from the rents received from your investment properties. Your goal is to own a number of homes free and clear—in other words, with the mortgage fully paid off—by the time you retire. In Chapter Two, I explained how to estimate the monthly income from a rental property. I'll recap it here, with a reminder that we're talking in **today's dollars**: over the years, these figures will rise along with the cost of living.

On a $135,000 home that rents for $1150 per month, there's a $750 per month profit once the mortgage is paid off. The other $400 goes toward recurring expenses, such as property tax, insurance, property management, vacancies and repairs. One free and clear home will net approximately $9000 per year. You can see how quickly this adds up:

1 home	$ 9,000 per year
2 homes	$ 18,000 per year
3 homes	$ 27,000 per year
4 homes	$ 36,000 per year
5 homes	$ 45,000 per year
6 homes	$ 54,000 per year
7 homes	$ 63,000 per year
8 homes	$ 72,000 per year
9 homes	$ 81,000 per year
10 homes	$ 90,000 per year
15 homes	$135,000 per year
20 homes	$180,000 per year

Once you've decided on the amount of annual income you'd like to have upon retirement, create a plan for buying properties. If you can buy multiple properties right away, that's terrific—you'll be well on your way to a great financial future. But perhaps you can only buy one right now. If that's true, then it's essential to make a financial plan to buy more properties in the future—a plan that's truly doable for you, one that you can accomplish and live with.

Following are scenarios of three different couples. Each couple was at a different stage in life, had different goals and financial requirements, but each couple was able to use real estate as a financial planning tool.

The charts accompanying the scenarios use a constant home price of $135,000, financed with an 30-year, fixed rate loan at 8% interest with 10% down. All figures except for those in the very last line are calculated in **today's dollars**, and have not been adjusted for inflation. The last line of the chart shows the amount of the amassed equity and projected income as a future value; in other words, after the value of today's dollars has been adjusted for inflation.

John & Susan: Scenario #1

John and Susan, age 30, initially purchased two homes that they intended to use to finance their children's college education. To build up equity faster, they made additional principal payments each year. After fifteen years, there was enough equity in the homes so that refinancing would provide plenty of cash for college expenses.

Five years after buying their first two homes, John and

Susan began buying homes for their retirement. At 35, they estimated that their retirement was thirty years away, so extra principal payments on these homes was not necessary. The income and the tax savings from their first two rental properties made it easier to save money each month—in fact, any profit after the extra principal payments were made was put into a money market account that was used to help save for a down payment on another property. In this way, they were able to buy one more property each year.

SCENARIO #1: JOHN & SUSAN			
Age		Equity	Income
30	Purchased 2 homes	$27,000	
35	Began buying 1 home per year	$92,016	
45	2 homes free & clear + 10 homes with various amounts of equity	$477,290	
45	Refinanced first 2 homes (2 new loans of $108,000 each)	$261,290	$216,000 (lump sum)
65	10 homes free & clear + 20 years of equity build-up in first 2 homes	$1,489,320 (today's $)	$90,000 per year (today's $)
FUTURE VALUE AT AGE 65: (with estimated 5% annual inflation)		$6,436,692 Equity	$388,971 Annual Income

All figures except for those in the very last line are calculated in today's dollars, and have not been adjusted for inflation. The last line of the chart shows the amount of the amassed equity and projected income as a future value; in other words, after the value of today's dollars has been adjusted for inflation.

By age 45, they owned 12 houses: 2 that were refinanced to provide for their children's education, and 10 that were held for their retirement. By age 65, they owned 10 houses free and clear, along with the first 2 houses they had purchased, which had built up another 20 years of equity.

As you can see from the figures below, John and Susan started out with a relatively low investment, approximately $30,000. By reinvesting their rental income and adding to it with their savings, they were able to pay off the first 2 houses in 15 years, and buy more houses. So, beginning with $30,000 they were able to pay for two four-year university stints, have a retirement income of $90,000 a year (in today's dollars), and own real property with a value of almost $1.5 million (in today's dollars).

Julie & Michael: Scenario #2

Julie and Michael, in their forties, had already set aside money for their children's education. Most of all, they needed to plan for their retirement, which they estimated was 20 years in the future. In addition, Julie hoped to someday change careers and start her own business.

They began by buying six homes, with five earmarked for retirement. The sixth house, which they planned to pay off in ten years, was set aside to finance Julie's business. Escalating rents made it possible to pay off the homes in 20 years—and for Julie and Michael to recoup their initial investment (and more) when they refinanced the sixth house only ten years after buying it. In this way, Julie was able to launch the business that she'd always dreamed of, without jeopardizing their retirement income.

SCENARIO #2: JULIE & MICHAEL			
Age		Equity	Income
45	Purchased 6 homes	$81,000	
55	1 home free & clear + equity in other 5 homes	$391,435	
55	Refinanced free & clear home (1 new loan of $108,000)	$283,435	$108,000 (lump sum)
65	5 homes free & clear + 10 years equity build-up in first home	$715,284 (today's $)	$45,000 per year (today's $)
FUTURE VALUE AT AGE 65: (with estimated 5% annual inflation)		$1,897,863 Equity	$119,399 Annual Income

All figures except for those in the very last line are calculated in today's dollars, and have not been adjusted for inflation. The last line of the chart shows the amount of the amassed equity and projected income as a future value; in other words, after the value of today's dollars has been adjusted for inflation.

Lisa & Lowell: Scenario #3

Lisa and Lowell, in their fifties, had less time to plan for their retirement than the two previous couples. However, being older, they had more cash available, and used it to make larger down payments on the 8 homes they purchased. Larger down payments meant smaller mortgages and higher profits from rental income. They used their profits to pay off the homes in ten years: at age 65, they owned property worth over $1 million (in today's dollars) which generated an annual income of $72,000 (in today's dollars).

SCENARIO #3: LISA & LOWELL			
Age		Equity	Annual Income
55	Purchased 8 homes with 30% down	$324,000	
65	8 homes free & clear	$1,080,000 (today's $)	$72,000 (today's $)
FUTURE VALUE AT AGE 65: (with estimated 5% annual inflation)		$1,759,212 Equity	$117,280 Annual Income

All figures except for those in the very last line are calculated in today's dollars, and have not been adjusted for inflation. The last line of the chart shows the amount of the amassed equity and projected income as a future value; in other words, after the value of today's dollars has been adjusted for inflation.

REPLAY

Purchasing multiple properties should be your ultimate goal.

Discuss your life goals and make a commitment to attaining them.

Choose an age at which you'd like to retire.

Estimate the number of properties you'll need.

Create a time-line for purchasing properties.

13

KEEPING TRACK OF YOUR INVESTMENTS

EVEN WHEN YOU OWN MULTIPLE PROPERTIES, THERE'S A SIMPLE system for charting income, expenses and other essential money-related issues that requires only a little of your time. For those who are computer-savvy, I've included some information on using Quicken as your accounting system, but you can get the job done with nothing more than a pencil, some paper, and a calculator.

Before you begin looking at the bottom line, however, you'll need to do two things: open a checking account and create a filing system.

Set Up a Separate Checking Account

Treat your real estate investment as a business, and keep it separate from your personal affairs. I strongly suggest opening a separate checking account used solely for rent deposits and mortgage payments. Even if you've only got one investment property, a separate account will help you keep track of investment income and expenses.

Organizing Documents

Purchasing property generates a lot of paper. If you've bought a house before, you already know about the tome-sized stack of documents you have to sign at closing. Included in this are the loan documents and various forms such as the Truth-in-Lending Act, Equal Opportunity Housing Act and Disclosure Statement.

Because the first (and the last) set of papers you'll keep are legal-size, I recommend buying a legal-size file cabinet, along with legal-size hanging files and manila file folders.

Create a Filing System

Each property should have its own separate hanging file, labeled with the property's address. Into this file goes that first sheaf of signed papers you brought home from the title company. Next, label a set of manila file folders with the following headings:

Rent Payments
Mortgage Payments
Property Management
Mortgage Statements
Repairs
Taxes
Insurance
Travel
Miscellaneous Expenses

These file folders should be kept in an adjacent hanging file (or two, if necessary), listed with the property's address, and should contain documents relating only to that property. Each property you own will require a set of the file folders listed above.

For the first file folder, Rent and Mortgage Payments, you'll need lined or graph paper to create a record of all transactions by month. If you owned the property for the entire year, begin with January. If you purchased the house later in the year, begin with the month in which you first paid the mortgage. For each month add these headings, left to right: Rent, Check Number, Date Deposited, Mortgage, Check Number, Date Paid, Profit/Loss.

A sample spreadsheet would look like this:

	RENT	CK#	DATE DEP.	MORT.	CK#	DATE PD.	P/L
Jan.				$896	289	1/15	<896>
Feb.	$1000	226	2/7/01	$896	325	2/15	$104
Mar.	$1000	237	3/7/01	$896	431	3/15	$104
Apr.	$1000	248	4/7/01	$896	485	4/15	$104
May	$1000	256	5/7/01	$896	515	5/15	$104
Jun.	$1000	278	6/7/01	$896	621	6/15	$104
Jul.	$1000	301	7/7/01	$896	646	7/15	$104
Aug.	$1000	322	8/7/01	$896	701	8/15	$104
Sep.	$1000	345	9/7/01	$896	736	9/15	$104
Oct.	$1000	369	10/7/01	$896	776	10/15	$104
Nov.	$1000	384	11/7/01	$896	825	11/15	$104
Dec.	$1000	410	12/7/01	$896	854	12/15	$104

In the above example, the property was purchased in January, and the first rental income was received in February. It's important to list all the months in which you paid the mortgage, not just the months in which you received rental income, so that you'll know how your expenses offset income at the end of the year.

If you have Excel or a similar software program, you can set up a spreadsheet that will calculate the profit or loss column for you (although a pencil and a calculator will do the job easily).

Filing Records and Receipts

In the **Property Management** folder, you'll keep the monthly and annual statements issued by the property management company. In the **Mortgage Statements** folder, file the monthly or quarterly statements issued by the lender, along with the year-end 1098 form, which shows the total principal, interest and property tax paid for the year. All receipts for repairs or any improvements should be kept in the **Repairs** folder. Under **Taxes**, file the county tax assessor's statements (even if property taxes are paid out of the escrow account, you'll receive a statement of property tax liability). All documents relating to the property's fire, hazard and liability insurance should be kept in the **Insurance** folder. Under **Travel**, file receipts for any expenses relating to travel to and from the property: air fare, car rental, and mileage log. Receipts for Federal Express, postage, or telephone can be filed under **Miscellaneous Expenses**.

The above system is very, very easy; once you've created

your file folders, your primary job is to make sure that the right documents get filed in the right folders. When tax time comes around, having your documents organized in this manner will make the task much easier.

As your portfolio grows, organizing all the papers, statements and receipts relating to your investments becomes increasingly important. Separate files for each property will prevent confusion later on. Even if you hold on to a property for 20 or 30 years, eventually you'll want to refinance, sell or exchange it, and you'll need to have the correct papers on hand.

Using Quicken as Your Accounting System

Setting up a computer program to record your income and expenses takes a little more time, but provides an accounting function that can handle all of the math for you, and offers the benefit of creating clear, concise reports and records for your files. In addition, you can transfer data from your Quicken account to your tax forms.

Even if you decide to use Quicken or a similar program to handle your accounting tasks, however, you'll still need to keep a paper file, as outlined above, for your documents and receipts.

Getting Started

First, you'll need to set up a Quicken account, the basic file in which you'll post income and expenses. It looks much like a check register and, in fact, will mirror your investment checking account. Upon setting up the account, you'll enter the date your investment checking account was opened, and the amount of your first deposit.

Next, choose **Classes** from the View menu, and click on **New** to enter the address of your investment property. You don't have to enter the entire address, just enough to distinguish it from other properties, i.e., "Elm St.," or "Palm Court."

Using the classes function in Quicken allows you to use one account to track all of your properties, yet separate them for individual reports.

After creating a class for each of your properties, you'll want to create a list of categories. Categories track income and expenses by type, just as your file folders keep different types of expenses separate from each other. Quicken offers a list of pre-set categories, but I recommend setting up a customized list that includes only the categories you'll need for your investment properties.

Choose **Categories and Transfers** from the View Menu, then click the **New** button that appears in the dialog box. For your first category, type in "Rent." Below the Category name field you'll see a box labeled **Type** and two buttons: **Income** and **Expense**. For the "rent" category, click on **Income**. "Rent" is the money that's flowing *into* your account. You may also want to create a second income category, called "Other Income" for any miscellaneous income items such as late fees from tenants, reimbursements, etc.

All other categories are **Expense** categories: the checks you write against the account. For each category, repeat this process: choose **Categories and Transfers** from the View

Menu, click the **New** button that appears in the dialog box, type in the name of the category, and click on **Expense**.

Create a list of the following categories (bold) and sub-categories (indented):

Mortgage Payment
> Principal and Interest
> Taxes
> PMI

Auto & Travel

Commissions

Insurance

Legal and other professional fees

Management Fees

Repairs

Supplies

Taxes

Utilities

Other

You can use the categories listed on Schedule E (Form 1040) of the tax return (see Chapter 14).

Entering Transactions

Just as you enter deposits and withdrawals to your checking account, you'll enter all transactions in your Quicken account. The difference is that, by assigning classes and categories to each entry, you'll be able to generate reports that can add up your income and expenses by class (individual property), and/or by category, such as the total amount of principal and interest paid to date.

As you work with Quicken, you may want to create more sub-categories to track your expenses, such as adding "Plumbing" or "Painting" under "Repairs." You can get as detailed as you like. The main thing, though, is to create categories that reflect the types of tax deductions you can take on your investment properties (I'll address that in detail in the next chapter).

Creating Reports

The time you spend entering data into your Quicken account will seem worthwhile once you see the result of your efforts printed out in a report. A report is, simply, a list of all transactions in either a class or a category. The report will add up all income and deduct expenses, giving you an instant bottom-line look at your investment.

Profit and Loss Statements

At the end of each year, you'll want to create a profit and loss statement. You can create a profit and loss statement for each property, or combine them for an overview of all your investments. If you've been diligent about filing all your documents and receipts in the correct folders, you'll have the necessary numbers at your fingertips.

On the facing page is an example of a P&L statement for a $100,000 property ($90,000 mortgage at 8%) that rents for $1000 a month.

PROFIT & LOSS STATEMENT

Income: (rent)	$12,000.00
Expenses:	
P&I:	<$ 7,924.00>
RE Taxes:	<$ 1,200.00>
PMI:	<$ 600.00>
Insurance:	<$ 500.00>
Prop. Mgmt.:	<$ 924.00>
Repairs:	<$ 500.00>
Misc.	<$ 120.00>
Total Expenses:	<$11,768.00>
Profit:	$ 232.00

Depreciation: Another Profit Booster

Let's assume that this $100,000 property has an improvement value of $80,000. The depreciation deduction would be approximately $2880 per year. When you add the depreciation deduction to the profit and loss statement, you can claim a loss of $2648. If you're in the 28% tax bracket, this represents a tax savings of $741. Together with the income from your rental property, you've made an after-tax profit of $973.

If you have an annual adjusted gross income of less than $100,000 per year, you can deduct losses of up to $25,000 each year. If your adjusted gross income is more than $100,000 per year, the amount you can deduct for losses is reduced according to income (see table in Chapter 14). However, even those with high incomes can gain tax benefits by carrying forward their losses into another year (again, see Chapter 14 for more information).

Updating Your Net Worth

Once you've completed your year-end profit and loss statement, you'll probably want to update your net worth worksheet.

How do your investments affect your net worth? One, by increasing the amount of cash on hand, in the form of profits from rentals and/or reduced taxes; and two, by appreciation and loan principal reduction, which create equity. These last two are elements that aren't typically noted on a profit and loss statement, and yet have great importance in terms of your net worth. Appreciation is the amount your property has increased in value. Equity is the difference between your loan balance and the property's market value.

Going back to the above example, let's assume you purchased the house in January and it's been rented for the entire year. You have already seen how you've made a profit of $973 ($232 in income, $741 in tax savings). The principal on the $90,000 loan, however, has been paid down to $89,280. The property has appreciated five percent, bringing its value up to $105,000. Your equity in the property is now $15,720: a $5,720 increase in one year.

Your $10,000 investment has increased your net worth by

$6693 in one year. That's almost a 67% return on your money. And keep in mind that the first year is usually the least profitable. As your property increases in value and rental prices rise (as, on average, they will with time), and the principal on the mortgage decreases at an ever-accelerating rate, your investment will reap far greater returns than this.

REPLAY

Open a separate checking account for rental income and mortgage payments.

Create a legal-size filing system.

Keep all income and expenses separated by property.

Use the **Classes** feature if you use Quicken to keep information on each property separate while using one account.

You can create a year-end profit and loss statement for each property, and/or combine for total profit and loss.

Add depreciation deduction to profit and loss figures for a look at your after-tax profits.

Include equity, attained by appreciation and loan principal reduction, in your updated net worth worksheet.

14

SELLING, REFINANCING, AND TAX-RELATED ISSUES

THERE WILL PROBABLY BE A TIME WHEN YOU'LL WANT TO SELL, refinance or trade one or more of your investment properties. Before taking this step, you'll need to know how this will affect your investment plan, income, and tax liability. In fact, I'm going to dive right into tax preparation in regard to your investment properties. Once you understand how rental income, deductions and depreciation affect your taxable income, you'll be able to make an informed decision about how to dispose of your property: whether to refinance, trade or sell.

Tax Preparation

The following is a general overview of current tax considerations. While this will give you an overall idea of how your real estate investments will affect your tax liability, I suggest using a tax preparer or a certified public accountant to prepare your tax return. Tax laws are subject to change from year to year, and you'll need someone who's up on all the latest revisions. In addition, the fee you pay for tax preparation is tax deductible.

Tax Deductions for Rental Properties

Income and expenses for rental properties are reported on Schedule E, Supplemental Income and Loss, and attached to your income tax return.

Each Schedule E (see illustration) provides space for three properties. If you own more than three, simply use as many Schedule E forms as necessary. In Part 1, list the street address, including city and state, and type of property, i.e., "4233 Oak Street, Dayton, Ohio, single family residence." On line 3, enter the total rents received for the tax year.

The primary expense categories are shown on lines 5 through 17:

Advertising

Any costs associated with advertising your rental, such as newspaper advertisements, "For Rent" signs, and Internet listings should be entered here. If you use a management company, the cost of advertising is included in the management fee, and should be reported under "Management fees" in line 11.

Auto and travel

All travel to and from your property, lodging, and 50% of your meal expenses while traveling can be deducted. You can also include any travel in connection with your rental activities, i.e., travel to and from a meeting with your property manager. For auto expenses, you can either deduct actual

SCHEDULE E (Form 1040) Department of the Treasury Internal Revenue Service (99)	**Supplemental Income and Loss** (From rental real estate, royalties, partnerships, S corporations, estates, trusts, REMICs, etc.) **Attach to Form 1040 or Form 1041.** **See Instructions for Schedule E (Form 1040).**	OMB No. 1545-0074 **2000** Attachment Sequence No. **13**

Name(s) shown on return

Your social security number

Part I **Income or Loss From Rental Real Estate and Royalties** Note. Report income and expenses from your business of renting personal property on **Schedule C** or **C-EZ** (see page E-1). Report farm rental income or loss from **Form 4835** on page 2, line 39.

1 Show the kind and location of each **rental real estate property:**	2 For each rental real estate property listed on line 1, did you or your family use it during the tax year for personal purposes for more than the greater of:		Yes	No
A --		A		
B --	14 days **or** 10% of the total days rented at fair rental value?	B		
C --	(See page E-1.)	C		

Income:		Properties			Totals (Add columns A, B, and C.)
		A	B	C	
3 Rents received . . .	3		3		
4 Royalties received . . .	4				4
Expenses:					
5 Advertising . . .	5				
6 Auto and travel (see page E-2) .	6				
7 Cleaning and maintenance . .	7				
8 Commissions . . .	8				
9 Insurance . . .	9				
10 Legal and other professional fees	10				
11 Management fees . . .	11				
12 Mortgage interest paid to banks, etc. (see page E-2) . . .	12				12
13 Other interest	13				
14 Repairs	14				
15 Supplies	15				
16 Taxes	16				
17 Utilities	17				
18 Other (list) ------------ ------------------- ------------------- -------------------	18				
19 Add lines 5 through 18 . .	19				19
20 Depreciation expense or depletion (see page E-3) . . .	20				20
21 Total expenses. Add lines 19 and 20	21				
22 Income or (loss) from rental real estate or royalty properties. Subtract line 21 from line 3 (rents) or line 4 (royalties). If the result is a (loss), see page E-3 to find out if you must file **Form 6198** .	22				
23 Deductible rental real estate loss. **Caution.** Your rental real estate loss on line 22 may be limited. See page E-3 to find out if you must file **Form 8582.** Real estate professionals must complete line 42 on page 2 . . .	23	( )	( )	( )	
24 **Income.** Add positive amounts shown on line 22. **Do not** include any losses . . .				24	
25 **Losses.** Add royalty losses from line 22 and rental real estate losses from line 23. Enter total losses here				25	( )
26 Total rental real estate and royalty income or (loss). Combine lines 24 and 25. Enter the result here. If Parts II, III, IV, and line 39 on page 2 do not apply to you, also enter this amount on Form 1040, line 17. Otherwise, include this amount in the total on line 40 on page 2				26	

For Paperwork Reduction Act Notice, see Form 1040 instructions. Cat. No. 11344L **Schedule E (Form 1040) 2000** expenses or the standard mileage rate. You must use actual expenses if you use more than one vehicle for your rental activities.

Cleaning and maintenance

Payments made for housecleaning services, landscape services, pool maintenance services, pest control, or other maintenance services (chimney sweep, rain gutter cleaning), should be reported here.

Commissions

If you sell your property, agent's commissions are entered here, along with lender commissions for refinancing.

Insurance

Under Insurance, include all premiums for fire, casualty and liability insurance.

Legal and other professional fees

Tax advice, tax preparation and costs incurred for tenant eviction would be entered here.

Management fees

Include all property management fees including fees for lease negotiation.

Mortgage interest

If you paid interest to a bank or other financial institution, you should receive a 1098 Form that shows the total interest paid for that year.

Other interest

If you received a loan from a friend or relative that was used to purchase the property, enter the total annual interest payment under "other interest." Be sure you have documentation—contract, and cancelled checks—to substantiate your deduction.

Repairs

According to the IRS, a repair is something that keeps your property in good working condition, but does not add significantly to its value or prolong its life. Conversely, a capital improvement increases the value of your property and extends its life.

If you use a property management company, they should provide you with an itemized list of all repairs made to your property. Enter the total amount spent for repairs.

Supplies

If you purchase cleaning supplies, tools, etc. for the maintenance of your property, you can deduct their actual cost.

Taxes

If taxes are paid from your escrow account, the amount paid will be itemized on the 1098 form you receive from the mortgage company. Otherwise, check the county tax assessor's statement for the total amount of taxes paid.

Utilities

You can deduct the cost of telephone calls related to your rental activities.

Depreciation

Depreciation is a deduction the government allows you to take to recover the cost of investment property that has a life beyond the tax year. For residential property, depreciation is deducted over a 27.5 year period. Land is not depreciable.

The amount of depreciation you may deduct is determined by the improvement value, which is the cost of the property less the cost of the land. Typically, the improvement value is figured at 50% to 80% of the property's total value.

The depreciation deduction is 3.636% (1/27.5) of the improvement value each year, except for the first year, which is pro-rated according to the month in which the property is first rented. In the first year, you can depreciate one-half of the first month the property was rented, regardless of which day it was occupied. For example, if you rent the property in June, your depreciation deduction would be 1.970% for that year.

1st YEAR DEPRECIATION PERCENTAGES

JAN	FEB	MAR	APR
3.485	3.182	2.879	2.576
MAY	JUN	JUL	AUG
2.273	1.970	1.667	1.364
SEP	OCT	NOV	DEC
1.061	0.758	0.455	0.152

Repairs and Capital Improvements

Repairs are fully deductible expenses defined, generally, as an expense to keep the property operational. Capital improvements increase the improvement value of the property, and lengthen its useful life.

For example, if you patch a hole in a wall, that's a repair; if you add a room with new walls, that's a capital improvement. Often, capital improvements can be depreciated over a period of five or seven years. This is an issue on which it's best to follow the advice of your tax preparer.

Profit and Loss

If your rental income is greater than your expenses and depreciation deduction, you'll show a profit that will be added to your taxable income, and entered on the 1040 form. If you have a loss, you'll be able to subtract it from your taxable income, with certain limitations.

Passive Activity Loss Rules

Rental real estate is considered a passive investment, and as such is subject to passive loss limitations. In general, this means that passive losses are deductible only against passive income, such as the income you earn from real estate. The tax law allows for certain exceptions, however; you can claim passive losses of up to $25,000 per year against your active income (wages, salary, etc.), if you meet the requirements for active participation. Happily, you can meet these requirements without regular or continuous involvement in your real estate activities, as long as you are responsible for significant decisions affecting your properties.

As defined by the IRS, you can meet the active participation requirements even when a property management company is handling your property, since you'll be making management decisions such as approving new tenants, deciding on rental terms, and authorizing capital or repair expenditures.

In addition to active participation, you must meet a few other requirements:

- **Rental real estate activities are your only passive activities.**

- **You do not have any prior year unallowed losses from passive activities.**

- **Your have no current or prior year unallowed credits from passive activities.**

- **Your modified adjusted gross income is $100,000 or less ($50,000 or less if married filing separately).**

If your modified adjusted gross income is $100,000 or less, you can deduct up to $25,000 in losses each year. If your modified adjusted gross income is more than $100,000, the amount of passive loss you can deduct is reduced incrementally according to income. Between $100,000 and $150,000, the passive loss exception is reduced 50 cents for every dollar your adjusted gross income exceeds $100,000 (see table on facing page).

Suspended Losses

If your adjusted gross income is more than $150,000, don't fret. If you're currently unable to claim passive losses against your active income, you can "carry forward" the losses from year to year.

Under current tax law, you can carry forward real estate investment losses indefinitely. The losses accrue each year, building up a kind of "savings account" of losses. When you

PASSIVE ACTIVITY LOSS ALLOWANCE

Income	Loss Allowance
$100,000	$25,000
$105,000	$22,500
$110,000	$20,000
$115,000	$17,500
$120,000	$15,000
$125,000	$12,500
$130,000	$10,000
$135,000	$7,500
$140,000	$5,000
$145,000	$2,500
$150,000	$0

sell or otherwise dispose of a property, these losses can be used to offset any gain.

Exception for Real Estate Professionals

If you work in a real estate trade or business at least 750 hours per year (about 14 hours per week), you are exempt from passive loss rules, and may deduct passive losses against your taxable income without limitations.

Essentially, this is a special tax-shelter for those in the real estate business, including real estate agents, loan brokers, property managers, and owners of rental properties. You don't need an agent's or broker's license, but you must meet the minimum annual hourly requirement. Also, more than one-half of the services you perform each year must fall within the definition of the real estate trade: buying and selling property, making loans, investing in properties, property management or construction.

Realizing Profits from Your Investments

When most people hear the word "profit" in conjunction with real estate investing, they assume it means selling property. But if you've followed the strategy put forward in this book, and have purchased relatively new, high quality properties in good markets and good locations, selling might be the least attractive method to realize gains from your investment.

Why? When you sell, three things happen:
- **You pay taxes**
- **You pay agents' commissions**
- **You lose an appreciating asset.**

For all of these reasons, selling incurs costs that can't be recovered. However, there are other ways to take cash out of your property or to leverage it for another investment without incurring all of these costs.

Refinancing

If you need cash for some reason—college tuition, or a major expense—refinancing or taking out an equity loan on your property offers a low-cost way to raise money. Interest on a new first mortgage, second mortgage or equity loan is tax-deductible, and the extra mortgage interest paid will offset your rental income. This will reduce the property's bottom line, and add less passive income to your earned income, which will reduce your taxes.

Here's an example of a typical property over 15 years, and

the monetary consequences of both selling and refinancing:

YEAR 2000

Original price:	$130,000
Loan amount:	$117,000 @ 8%
Monthly payments:	$858.50 (principal and interest)
	$150.00 (taxes)
	$ 80.00 (PMI)
	$ 50.00 (insurance)
	$ 60.00 (prop. management)
TOTAL:	$1198.50
Monthly Rent:	$1200.00

As you can see, this property started out with a slight positive monthly cash flow of $1.50 a month, which adds up to an annual positive cash flow of $18. With the annual depreciation deduction of approximately $3600, however, you can declare a loss of $3582. If you're in the 28% tax bracket, that's an in-your-pocket profit of $1003 the first year—which raises the positive cash flow to $83.58 per month.

After 15 years, the numbers on the property undergo a profound change:

YEAR 2015	
Original price:	$130,000
Current value:	$270,257 (rising 5% annually)
Original Loan:	$117,000 @ 8%
Loan balance:	$89,856
Monthly payments:	$ 858.50 (principal and interest)
	$ 312.00 (taxes - rising 5% annually)
	$ 104.00 (ins. - rising 5% annually)
	$ 150.00 (prop. management)
TOTAL:	$1424.50
Monthly Rent:	$2495 (rising 5% annually)
Equity:	$180,462

After 15 years, the property has built up nearly $200,000 in equity and is generating profits of $1070.50 per month, or $12,846 per year. (Note there's no longer a PMI payment.) But now you want to cash out. How much money will you actually receive?

Let's assume the house sells for its current market price of

$270,000. After paying off the balance of the original loan, you're left with capital gains of approximately $180,000.

The new capital gains rate (for property purchased after January 1, 2000), is 18%. This is a favorable rate compared to capital gains tax in past years; however, not all states are compliant with capital gains tax rates. For example, California does not use capital gains tax rates: all capital gains are taxed as income, according to your tax bracket. As we all know, taxes are the first thing to come straight off the top of your profit: you must assume that 18% is the very least you'll pay. So your $180,000 is reduced (at least) $32,400 by capital gains taxes.

In addition, you must pay taxes on depreciation recapture: the depreciation that you have deducted over the past fifteen years is added up and taxed at 25% (unless you're in the 15% tax bracket, in which case depreciation recapture is taxed at 10%). For the above example, the depreciation deductions taken over 15 years add up to $19,833 (assuming an improvement value of $100,000). A 25% tax on this amount is $4958.

You will also pay agents' commissions (6%), which on a $270,000 sale is $16,200.

So what do you have left over after the sale is final? $126,442.

Certainly, $126,442 in the hand is better than a kick in the head but, at a minimum, you'll spend $50,000 to get it. Last but not least: you no longer have an appreciating asset, one that could, in the next ten to fifteen years, rise in value another $200,000 or more.

In contrast, here's what happens when you refinance:

YEAR 2015

Original price: $130,000
Current value: $270,257
Original Loan: $117,000 @ 8%
Orig. loan balance: $89,856
New Loan: $190,000 @ 8%

Monthly payments: $1394.00   (new loan P & I)
                   $ 312.00   (taxes - rising 5% annually)
                   $ 104.00   (ins. - rising 5% annually)
                   $ 150.00   (prop. management)

TOTAL: $1960
Monthly Rent: $2495
Monthly Profit: $ 535

Cash Out: $100,000
Equity: $80,462

Even with the new mortgage payment, the property has a positive monthly cash flow of $535, or $6420 each year. And since your depreciation deduction is still $3600, you'll be able to reduce your taxable income to $2820.

For a cost of three to five percent of the loan amount (in the above example, about $3000 to $5000), you've raised $100,000 on which you don't have to pay taxes. You also have $80,000 equity remaining in the property, and an appreciating asset that will continue to generate profits, tax savings, and increase your net worth.

Trading to Defer Taxes: The 1031 Exchange

In a tax-deferred exchange, real property can be traded without tax liability. In other words, instead of selling your property and paying taxes, you can use all of the equity in your property to trade for another property or properties, without taking the big tax bite (until the later sale of the replacement property). You can think of it as an equity preservation program that works through reinvestment.

Typically, the person you sell property to is not the one you're buying from, which means that most exchanges are really three party affairs: you, the person who buys your property, and the person you buy property from. Once your property is sold, you have 45 days in which to identify a replacement property, and 180 days to complete the acquisition of the property.

There are a few parameters that must be adhered to:

- **Traded properties must be of "like kind."** This rule is interpreted broadly, but it generally means that both properties must be properties held for investment or for use in one's trade or business.

- **Property acquired must be of equal or greater value to**

the net sale price of property sold. (The "net sale price" is the sale price minus closing costs and broker's fee.)

- **Properties must be in the U.S.**

- **Typically, the entire net sale proceeds go towards the acquisition of the replacement property.** In cases where the exchanger receives cash, personal property or other assets in the exchange, it is taxable.

- **An intermediary is used to facilitate the exchange and hold funds during the period between sale and acquisition.** The exchanger is not allowed possession of the funds in the interim.

The point of the 1031 exchange is to avoid depletion of the equity you've already built up, and to avoid capital gains tax. The 1031 exchange allows you to reinvest that equity without paying taxes, as long as you do it within a specific time frame, and according to specific rules. The rules for tax-deferred exchanges can be complex and exacting, so it's best to consult a specialist before moving ahead. That said, it's an excellent way to rollover your equity into another investment; for example, to trade in an older property for a newer one that will have greater depreciation, a longer functional life, fewer repairs, and higher rental rates. You can also use equity from one property to reinvest in several properties, or consolidate several less expensive properties into a more expensive one.

Selling Your Property

I've saved selling for last because, in my view, there are only a few good reasons to sell an investment property. The benefits of holding onto the property—or refinancing or exchanging it—are often greater in the long run. However, there are some circumstances under which you may find it prudent to sell your property.

It's a Dog: It's a fact of life that some properties are bad. If you're having a hard time keeping it rented, it needs lots of repairs, and you're losing money, get rid of it.

You Need Cash: If, for some reason, you need an instant influx of all the money you can get your hands on, you may have no choice but to sell.

Suspended losses: If you have been unable to claim passive losses because of a high taxable income, and these losses will greatly reduce the amount of capital gains realized from the sale, selling may be more to your advantage than refinancing or exchanging.

REPLAY

Gain a thorough understanding of rental property tax law to make the most of deductions and depreciation.

Use a tax preparer or CPA who has a knowledge of real estate tax law to prepare your tax return.

If your adjusted gross income is under $100,000, you can deduct up to $25,000 a year in passive losses against active income.

Suspended losses can be "rolled-over" indefinitely, and subtracted from capital gains realized from sale of property.

Real estate professionals can claim unlimited losses.

Selling your property incurs unrecoverable costs.

Refinancing offers tax-free cash.

Consider a 1031 exchange before selling.

GLOSSARY

Adjustable Rate Loan

An adjustable rate loan, or ARM, is a loan with a variable interest rate that rises or falls according to the index to which it is tied.

Adjusted Gross Income

Your taxable income after deductions.

Annual Percentage Rate

The annual percentage rate, or APR, reflects the true annual cost of a loan. The APR is determined by adding the interest rate and loan fees, and is expressed as a percentage.

Appraisal

An estimate of property value produced by an independent appraiser.

Appreciation

The increase of property value.

Capital Gains

Capital gains are the taxable profits derived from the sale or exchange of a capital asset, such as real property.

Capital Improvement

Capital improvements increase the value of property. For

the depreciation schedules of various capital improvements, check with your tax preparer.

Cash Flow

Cash flow is the difference between expenses and income. For example, if a property has an income of $10,000 and expenses of $4000, it has a $6000 positive cash flow. If expenses are $12,000, it has a $2000 negative cash flow.

Closing

Also known as "settlement." Closing is the act of finalizing all arrangements between the buyer and seller. Money is disbursed, the deed is prepared in the new owner's name, and the property is conveyed in accordance with the contract signed by both parties.

Closing Costs

The fees associated with the closing of escrow, or of a loan.

Contingencies

Also known as conditions of sale, contingencies are conditions that, if not met, ensure that the sale will not go through. For example, if the property inspection report reveals property damage, you will be able to cancel the sale.

Depreciation

Depreciation is for tax-purposes-only loss against the property, prorated over 27.5 years for residential property.

Equity

Equity is the cash value of a property, less any outstanding mortgages and liens.

Escrow

Escrow is a trust account wherein deposit money is held by a neutral third party (usually an escrow officer or title company) prior to finalization of the sale. When escrow is "closed," it means that the transaction has been completed: the seller is paid and the buyer takes title to the property.

Fixed-rate Loan

A fixed-rate loan has an interest rate that does not change over the life of the loan.

Flip

To "flip" a property is to sell it soon after buying it.

Foreclosure

Foreclosure goes into effect when the property owner defaults on the mortgage and the lender takes possession of the property.

Hybrid Loan

A hybrid loan combines an adjustable-rate loan and fixed-rate loan.

Improvement Value

When you take a depreciation deduction, you may only take depreciation against the cost of the structure, not the land. The structure is also known as the "Improvements." The improvement value is the cost of the property less the cost of the land.

Interest

Interest is what lenders charge for the use of their money.

Interest is expressed as a percentage, or interest rate.

Leverage

Leverage means to borrow and use other people's money, generally a bank's or lending institution's.

Lien

A lien is a claim against property, which can include mortgages, trusts, and unpaid property taxes. The primary purpose of a title search is to be certain that all liens are known at the day of settlement.

Market

A market is an area, usually defined by city, in which to invest.

Median Price

The median price is the result of averaging the property prices in a given market, in which the prices of recently sold homes are added together and divided by the number of homes sold. For example, the median price for a market in which one home sold for $100,000 and another home sold for $600,000 would be $350,000. The median price for a market in which one home sold for $100,000 and two homes sold for $600,000 would be $433,333.

Net Worth

Net worth is the wealth you've accumulated to date, i.e., what's left after subtracting your liabilities from your assets.

No Money Down

"No Money Down" can also be thought of as 100 percent

financing. If you borrow money for the down payment, then you have purchased a property with 100 percent financing, or no money down.

Passive Loss Allowance

If your modified adjusted gross income is less than $100,000 per year, you can claim up to $25,000 in passive losses each year.

Points

A point is an up-front fee paid to the lender at closing. One point equals one percent of the loan amount; e.g., one point of a $100,000 loan would be $1000.

Principal

The principal is the loan amount, which is paid off in part each month along with the interest payment.

Private Mortgage Insurance, or PMI

When you make a down-payment of less than 20%, lenders require that you carry private mortgage insurance, or PMI. PMI protects lenders from financial loss if the homeowner goes into foreclosure.

Profit & Loss Statement

A profit and loss statement is an accounting of your investment's income and expenses, which will show either profit or loss.

Property Inspector

Property inspectors are hired by potential home buyers to evaluate the physical state of a property before its purchase.

Property Manager

For a fee, generally between six and nine percent of the gross rent collected, a property manager can handle all aspects of renting and maintaining your investment property, from leasing to repairs.

Real Estate Facilitator

A real estate facilitator coordinates real estate investments for private investors. A facilitator locates property, negotiates the purchase price, arranges financing, expedites the paperwork and sets up property management.

Refinance

To refinance means to secure new financing for a property, whether by securing a new first mortgage or an equity or second mortgage.

Repair

Repairs are fully deductible expenses for items and services that keep the property operational.

Retirement Account

A retirement account is a long-term savings and investment account. Popular retirement accounts include IRAs, 401(k)s and Keogh plans.

Return

Return is the amount of profit realized from an investment. For example, if you make $4000 on a $10,000 investment, that's a 40% return.

Single Family Home

A single family home is single unit, detached dwelling with a yard.

Suspended Losses

If your adjusted gross income is more than $150,000 each year, you can carry forward passive losses to future years, building up a kind of "savings account" of losses that can be used to offset capital gains.

INDEX

REMOTE CONTROLLED
REAL ESTATE RICHES

ORDER FORM

PHONE: 1-800-324-3983   FAX: 415-924-7869
(Fax this form)

POST: Progress Press
      101 Lucas Valley Rd. Suite 130
      San Rafael, CA 94903
EMAIL: ppress@webperception.com

Please send _____ copy/copies of
      Remote Controlled Real Estate Riches
      @ $21.95 each

Shipping (U.S.): $4.00 for first book; $2.00 for each additional book. International: Please contact us for rates. Sales Tax: Please add 7.5% tax for books shipped to California addresses. Please make checks payable to ICG.

TOTAL AMOUNT ENCLOSED: $_____

Please send FREE information on:
_____Seminars/Lectures   _____Consulting

Name:_____
Address:_____
City_____State:_____Country:_____
Zip/Postal Code:_____
Telephone:_____Email:_____